THE STARS

THE

STARS

BY RICHARD SCHICKEL

designed by

ALLEN HURLBURT

BONANZA BOOKS • NEW YORK

This guide to a most peculiar American institution is dedicated to Susan Hurlburt and to Samuel and Matthew Whedon, three small strangers in our land, in hopes that it will help them to understand what in the world their parents are talking about.

FOREWORD

This book is an impressionistic rather than an exhaustive history of the institution of movie stardom. Literally hundreds of men, women, children and animals have, at one time or another, received billing above the title of a film and are thus entitled, by the broadest possible definition, to the appellation "star." Our criteria in the selection of names to be included in this study have been, perforce, much narrower than that. In general, we have striven to give most space to that handful of people who have been superstars, personalities who have dominated the screen for long periods of time and who, by the force of their presence, have altered the nature of screen content. Of those stars whose course was briefer, but whose light was sometimes more intense, we have tried to include people who were peculiarly representative of the nation's mood at a given moment or who answered some particularly pressing socio-psychological need. At this level our choice was wider and we were guided partly by the availability of good photographs and partly by personal taste. It is especially true of this subject that individuals develop strange attractions to unlikely performers, equally inexplicable dislikes for others. Both author and designer have tried to keep the expression of their own eccentricities of taste to a minimum. But it is only fair to say that in those instances when everything else was equal, we chose to include the actor or actress we had—or have— a sneaking fondness for.

As to our general purpose, the book itself should make that clear. We believe that the picture-book form is peculiarly suited to this subject and, however frequently the form has been misused in the past, we believe that it is possible to make serious statements through the intelligent use of it. Though we believe the book to be both beautiful and amusing, we also hope, through the use of the star as metaphor, we have said something useful about the social history of our times and, certainly, about the history of a medium that has been the most important purveyor of popular culture in this century. Indeed, we hope that we have redressed an imbalance that has existed for a long time in serious writing about the films. Most critics have concentrated on the contributions of the director to the developing aesthetic of movies. This is, of course, the best way to approach European films, as well as American films made before the rise of the studio system in Hollywood. It may again become, in this day of independent production, the best way of dealing with American film history. But from, roughly, 1920 to 1950, American films, for the most part, have been tailored to fit the special talents of their stars. The presence of those stars together with the commercial judgment of the producers—a judgment that, to say the least, is not always sound—has, more than any other single factor, determined what we see. It is the specific nature of this influence that we attempt to demonstrate in this book.

The careful reader will be aware of the author's debt to several critics and commentators. So that there can be no doubt as to his intellectual mentors, he would like to list them here and pay tribute to their benign influence on his thinking and writing. They are: James Agee, Manny Farber, Parker Tyler, Kenneth Tynan and Robert Warshow. On specific points each and all of them have guided me, but more important, their shared attitude, which is one of love for the movies, not cultural superiority toward them, has been of great comfort to me.

The Stars could not have been produced without access to two fine collections of stills, one belonging to the Museum of Modern Art and the other to Culver Pictures. We wish to thank these institutions and their dedicated employees for their aid. Thanks are due also to several private collections whose aid has been invaluable to us. The author's special gratitude is directed toward his wife, Julia Whedon Schickel, who not only did the major share of our basic picture research, but also undertook dozens of the essential chores of fact-finding and organization, served as a sounding board for ideas and, most important of all, bore with patience, fortitude and a sense of humor, the writer's grumpy manner of working. She has always loved the movies almost as much as I do. I hope she still does.

RICHARD SCHICKEL

New York

CONTENTS

INTRODUCTION

MANY INTELLIGENT PEOPLE are vaguely suspicious of the movies. Movies, they say, are not "serious." Nevertheless— and unfortunately—they go to the movies. They can't help themselves; they need the comforting darkness, the abandonment of reality, the startling immediacy of fantasy which can be found at the neighborhood movie house. But films being *declassé*, these people have had to discover cultural attitudes to legitimatize their attendance. They have found two. One is the insistence that movies are art and going to see them is a quest for aesthetic enlightenment on the same level as theatergoing, gallery-trotting or the reading of Henry James. The other, wrapped in the warmly protective cloak of social science, is the view that the film is a way of sampling public opinion; at the movies, it claims, you can measure popular sexual attitudes, the level of unconscious violence in the society, even the shifts in the sociopolitical wind.

Both of these attitudes have been productive, at their best, of some provocative writing, but neither has given a total picture of the *experience* of the movies as most of us understand it. It is almost impossible to retain critical objectivity about the movies. It is the nature of the medium to hit below the belt. One is drawn into a film in such a way that visceral responses quite overcome critical faculties. All is lost, save attitudes which are hastily readjusted, once the film is over, much in the way the clothes of teen-age lovers are readjusted—hastily, and with a great pretense of nonchalance—when a cop's flashlight suddenly shines through the window of the parked car.

In short, the attitudes we take to the movies generally prevent us from fully understanding what we see and even

The old Hollywood meets the new, in the best movie about movies ever made, Sunset Boulevard. *In a projection room Gloria Swanson, as the forgotten star, recalls her youth and that of Hollywood for William Holden. In their styles, director Billy Wilder found the perfect contrast between the old grand manner and the new naturalism. The film they are watching is* Queen Kelly, *a 1930 Swanson film, directed by Erich Von Stroheim, but never released by Paramount.*

prohibit the full enjoyment of the film. Nowhere is this more apparent than in serious discussions of the role of the movie star in film history. As we shall shortly see, the star stands at the very center of movie economics (at least in America, which has no tradition of the art film) and it is to his public image that all movies, no matter how high their professed artistic aims, are tailored. Yet one can read essay after essay, book after book, and find nothing about stars more pertinent than brief discussions of performances, couched in the inapplicable terms of the stage. Serious and semiserious discussions all revolve around the question of whether X is a good actor, or whether he is an actor at all. The position of this book is that the question is irrelevant. Movie stars are not usually, or necessarily, actors; they are . . . movie stars. The two occupations are entirely different, although they are sometimes compatible.

Further, the importance of the star to the movies has changed the very nature of the individual film product. "The growth of the film personality," says Frank Getlein, "meant the death of the movie as one of the fictional arts. The two ideas are in violent opposition; the personality eliminates the director and substitutes the publicity man as the guiding force in film making; and the creation and merchandising of daydreams is a direct contradiction of the art of fiction." Obviously the theories of film aestheticians, which revolve around the skill of the director in creating art works to be judged by the conventional standards of fiction, are rendered meaningless in this context. The social psychologists concentrate too heavily on film content, too little on the nature of the personalities which shape that content.

This book is an attempt to redress that balance. Generally speaking, the author devotes the greater share of his effort to extracting from films the essence of the personalities for which they were vehicles rather than to the content and intent of the vehicle itself. In these essences, I feel, lies a great deal (but not all) of the truth about the non-art of the movies. The book takes no moral position about whether American movies would have been better or worse had they not succumbed to the cult of personality. All we can say for certain is that they would have been different.

It may comfort those who regard the star system as a sin and a shame to know that it was created by popular demand, over the objections of the pioneering movie moguls. Stars apparently answered a deeply felt human need, but these needs were not in the beginning and are not to this day exploited with any great cleverness by the movie makers. Star quality being such an elusive and ill-defined thing, film producers have always operated on a cafeteria basis, placing before the public any number of tasty morsels, then sitting back to see which of them the public hungers for most deeply. One of the surprising things anthropologist Hortense Powdermaker discovered when she investigated Hollywood was that "there is rarely a well-thought-out program of how a studio could make a good star." Selection is usually—but not always—left to chance, and more often than not the movie men themselves are surprised by its workings. They were similarly surprised, in the beginning, by the potential of the star system, by the strength of the bond that was created between stars and audience.

In the beginning, there were no such things as stars. In the Nickelodeon Era, when the production end of the industry was located in New York, it was almost impossible to get stage actors of any kind, stars or not, to work in the movies. Salaries were infinitesimal, prestige non-existent. Those crude geniuses of fast-dollar finance who controlled the infant industry found a style they considered suitably broad and a refreshing eagerness to work for five or ten dollars a day among unemployed bit players and vaudevillians. They became the backbone of an industry determined to maximize profits by producing on the cheap. Hangdog, the actors crept, under the cover of assumed names, out to Fort Lee, New Jersey, there to sit uneasily on horses during the production of Westerns, or to the wilds of the Bronx or Brooklyn, or to downtown Manhattan, where the comedies and dramas of social conscience (usually about the perils of drink or of the evils which might befall the innocent working girl) were shot.

The public for these films was a gloriously innocent one, made up chiefly of immigrants and other members of the lower economic orders. For them, lack of sound and the resulting lack of subtle ideas were a positive boon. For once they could relax in comforting darkness and abandon their struggles with that most intractable of tongues— English. In an atmosphere redolent of sweat and cheap perfume, for the price of a nickel, they were able to participate in fantasies of the most satisfying kind. Since it was obligatory that the endings of these little films be happy, with the man or woman of the people emerging triumphant over the uniformly sappy representatives of privilege, a curious phenomenon began to take place. The canaille began to identify with both the sufferings and the triumphs of their screen counterparts. And by 1910, letters addressed to "The Waif" or "The Man with the Sad Eyes" began to trickle into the studios.

Florence Lawrence, the first Biograph girl, was rescued from anonymity by Carl Laemmle and, in 1910, became the first modern style movie star. Her star career was brief and she ended up, in the thirties, playing bits.

This development caused great alarm to the men in control of the studios, particularly those who had joined with Thomas Edison in the so-called trust, a generally unsuccessful attempt to limit the production of films. If the actors learned that the public had singled out certain members of the fraternity for special favor, they would undoubtedly begin to demand more money for their services, thereby upsetting the delicate economic balance of the industry.

As if this were not bad enough, the industry was harboring in its midst a saboteur of the conventional wisdom. D. W. Griffith, a reformed actor with literary aspirations, began to direct films for Biograph in 1908. The Biograph years were, for Griffith, ones of experiment, learning how to break all the old, static rules of movie making, teaching the camera to move, learning how to edit his film in order to create the illusion of life's rhythm rather than that of the stage. In the course of creating for the film a new basic grammar, Griffith kept moving his camera closer, ever closer to the faces of his actors. He quickly discovered its cruelty, particularly in those days of flat, harsh lighting and bad film. He needed unlined, youthful faces for his close-ups, just as he needed unwrinkled minds which he could command absolutely. He had no need of older actors, set in their ways and impervious to his imperious ego. He therefore built a stock company of malleable, youthful players, among them Blanche Sweet, Mae Marsh, Mabel Normand, Linda Arvidson (Griffith's wife), Lillian and Dorothy Gish, and Florence Lawrence, perhaps the least important talent of the group, but a girl who was shortly to play a revolutionary role in movie history.

Thus the stage was set for the emergence of the beautiful people, the stars. The public had begun to find them out, despite the best efforts of the industry to conceal their identities. And within the industry a new way of making films was creating a genuine artistic demand for youth and beauty.

It remained only for Carl Laemmle to put the two demands together and create that strange being we know today as the Movie Star. The instrument of his will was Miss Florence Lawrence, already a minor celebrity as the original Biograph girl. In 1910 Laemmle offered Miss Lawrence a thousand dollars a week for her exclusive services to IMP (Independent Motion Picture Company). He launched her into starry orbit with characteristic dash. Shortly after signing her, he planted a fake story in the press stating that Miss Lawrence had been killed beneath the wheels of a trolley car in St. Louis. Then he rushed into print crying not merely that the report was grossly exaggerated, but that it was, indeed, the work of the monstrous movie trust, just one more example of the lengths to which it would go to crush its struggling competition. Miss Lawrence, cried Laemmle, was in flourishing health and, to prove it, she would visit St. Louis, accompanied by her leading man, King Baggott. All and sundry were invited to come down to the station to see for themselves that she was as alive and lovely as ever. Hundreds turned out for the first personal appearance in movie history and admirers "demonstrated their affection by tearing the buttons off Florence Lawrence's coat, the trimmings from her hat, the hat from her head."

Within a year, the stock company Griffith had built at Biograph was partly destroyed by the independents, who were quick to follow Laemmle's lead. In the somehow charming jungle that was the movie business in its early days, vigorous and wildly aggressive companies that existed outside the trust (and outside the written, if not the moral, law) were in desperate need of any competitive edge they could seize. The creation and marketing of stars was such an edge. Indeed, it is not too much to say that the creation of the star system was the chief factor in the transformation of the movie business from a struggling, squabbling collection of small concerns into the monolithic industry which it was at the height of its power.

Stars gave to the business the stability of mass production. You could predict very closely the probable profits of a major star's vehicle, and it was like money in the bank to know that you had a number of such items in various stages of production. You merely kept grinding them out, sure in the knowledge that, if you didn't radically change the formula, profits would follow as the night the day. Thus did production line methods come to the movies just as new methods of distribution, through nationwide chains of exchanges, were creating a need for standardized mass-produced products. Three years after the historic Florence Lawrence publicity coup, everyone had taken to the star system, the first fan magazine (owned by Vitagraph) had begun publication, and the mills of personal publicity had begun their inexorable grind.

The first stars, as noted, had been created by the public. Through the mysterious process known as identification, large numbers of people had come to see something of themselves (or, at least, the fantasy image of themselves) in various screen personalities. And, in the period between 1910 and 1920, the great prototype screen personalities began to appear. These stars were archetypes, all unaware of the common chord they set reverberating in millions of people.

They became models for hundreds who were to follow.

Of them, the Keystone Kops, William S. Hart, Mary Pickford and Douglas Fairbanks were, in a sense, originals. Only one of the great prototypes, Theda Bara, was a totally made-up creature, the "invention" of William Fox. She was a little Ohio girl who, through adroit make-up, careful selection of stories and, most importantly, a spectacular publicity campaign, was transformed into a symbol of exotic sexuality, a figure, indeed, so exaggerated as to be comically grotesque. She was, as they say, just *too much*, and she was rather quickly laughed off the screen. But as a totally fabricated personality, she represented a radical reversal of what, for the first few years of the star system, had been the usual way of doing business. Until then, the creation of stars had been a fairly natural phenomenon; an actor would be noticed by the public in a small part, his talents would be nurtured and publicized by a shrewd studio and, finally, in the good old American pluck-and-luck way, he would achieve his peculiar destiny—movie stardom. Now, following the lead of William Fox, the moguls realized that the process could be reversed— the public could be made to accept, through the assiduous use of publicity techniques, almost anyone the studios thought they should. At least, this was the opinion of two disparate groups, cynics within the industry and the ever-poised moralists and intellectual critics to whose voluminous recordings of every Hollywood mistake, failure and lapse of taste all of us owe so much.

In point of fact, it is extremely difficult to make a great star out of ordinary clay. It has been done, but it is not easy. And Hollywood is strewn with the wreckage of careers for which a flourish of expertly beaten drums was sent rolling across the land, but which failed to make it with the public. For proof one need only glance at the career of Marion Davies, whom all the millions of Hearst and M-G-M could not make a truly first-rate star, or at Vera Hruba Ralston, who was married to Herbert Yates, president of Republic Pictures. Mr. Yates did everything he could for his wife, soaring far above and beyond the call of connubial duty. The result was nothing short of disastrous. And when; a few years ago, a group of stockholders sought to oust Mr. Yates from control of his studio, one of the chief charges brought against his management was this expensive bit of nepotism. Yates lost his job.

So, it is almost impossible to create demand for an individual star when none exists in the unconscious minds of the audience. But the demeaning ordeals through which the would-be star is put by an industry which is particularly brutal in pursuit of profits has had its effect. Simply put, it has made the task of being a star incredibly difficult in terms

of its demands on psychological stamina. In addition, there is the problem of survival.

Anxiety is the feeling of powerlessness in circumstances beyond the control of the individual. No one is less powerful than a film star in the face of sudden public indifference to his art or his charms. He must live under the constant threat that the audience may turn away from him. It takes a more than usually powerful ego to live successfully with that threat, especially in an industry which, according to Hortense Powdermaker, is at great pains, for reason of deep envy, to demean the star. They are, she says, "looked down upon as a kind of sub-human species. No one respects them. . . . They are often described as children who don't know what is good for them, immature, irresponsible, completely self-centered, egotistical, exhibitionistic, nitwits, and utterly stupid." She adds, rather dryly, "Part of this description is reminiscent of white attitudes in the Deep South toward Negroes." No wonder that in recent years stars have been tumbling over one another in their eagerness to set up their own production companies. There are sound tax· and business reasons for this, of course, but there is another—improved status. The fight for human dignity takes some strange turns.

Since it is currently fashionable to do so, let us take a middle-of-the-road position. Some stars are indeed "immature" (et cetera), and some are not; but all are cursed with having to contend with our strange ambivalence toward them and their work. Miss Powdermaker observes that "in primitive society there is a deep biological tie between the people and their mythical heroes, since these are also their ancestors. They are important to all members of the clan or tribe, young and old, and the myths and folk tales about them serve as sanctions for behavior and customs." This is the beginning of wisdom about stars and their value to us as individuals.

But it is hard wisdom to accept. People who don't like movies, or who take an attitude of either cultural or moral superiority toward them, accept the idea gleefully enough.

But the average person is unconsciously resentful of this knowledge. Its implication is that he has need of false gods, gods which will bring him gifts of pleasure that he is incapable of securing for himself through his own imagination. This may account for his love-hate relationship with his stars. Something within him responds mightily to their presence; he can't help that. But something, possibly our culture, tells him that this should not be so. He is angry with what he thinks of as his own weakness, transfers this anger to his favorites, but holds it in check until they make some kind of misstep, either on screen or in their personal lives. Then his scornful anger knows no bounds, and no punishment is too great for the transgressors. He may emulate their behavior, their style, for a time, but he is always waiting for the moment when he can smite down his gods.

This was particularly true in the days of the silent screen. At that time, the stars were much more abstractions than they were real people. They personified, each in his different way, ideas or ideals, just as Greek gods were personifications of the great virtues. If one of them fell from grace, as several did during the wave of Hollywood scandals early in the twenties, it was not just a personal tragedy, it was a calling into question of an entire concept of behavior, a large chunk of the moral code by which the nation lived.

This remained true as long as the screen was silent. A godhead is supposed to be inscrutable; it is not expected that he speak directly to us. It is enough that his image be present so that we may conveniently worship it. In those days it was expected that the stars would lead lives as different as possible from those of ordinary mortals. And, although they might be mobbed on occasion when they ventured out in public, and although they were expected to contribute their mite, whenever possible, to the rumor mills, they were also expected to keep their distance. The public wanted them to be different, and they were. The publicity of the age was different in quality from that which we have grown used to. Its very hokiness raised it, on occasion, to rare levels of amusement, and the public was seldom subjected to the drool about stars' family life, religious beliefs, theories of child rearing and the other homey, we're-just-like-you nonsense that is *de rigueur* today. Indeed, stars went to considerable lengths to conceal wives and children, fearing that these represented fan-shattering descents into the ordinary.

The movie star was brought down to earth by the combined impact of social and technological change. Sound came to the movies only months before the depression came to America. The former revolutionized the industry, of course, just as the latter precipitated a radical revision of social values. It now became necessary to prove that stars were just like everyone else, only more so. It is doubtful that Marion Davies painted over her 14-carat gold ceiling or that Gloria Swanson actually gave up dunking herself in the solid-gold bathtub that was the focal point of her black-marble bathroom, but the publicity departments turned the attention of the public away from such didoes, and directed it toward the more human side of the stars' lives. Public information on salaries, mansions, wardrobe, and so on, diminished, and a new kind of star came to the screen. The age of the American hero, tough, cynical, wise-cracking, frequently unchivalrous toward women, was upon us. Gone were the Latin lovers; gone, for the most part, were the vamps, the sloe-eyed sensualists who had tempted many a good American boy to his doom on the silent screen. Even the virginal staple underwent a transformation. She did not lose her virtue, but she did tend to be a good deal more knowledgeable about the world and its ways than the Gish sisters or Mary Pickford had been. More than one commentator has noted that when James Cagney pushed the grapefruit into Mae Clark's face in *Public Enemy*, screen love and, for that matter, screen manners changed forever. Certainly the moment is one of those bench marks in social history that cannot be ignored.

The exuberant romanticism of the twenties was, at that moment, destroyed forever. And so, too, was the decent distance between star and audience. Now that they were playing parts which, at least in the details of dress, manner and speech, were intended to resemble the lives of their audience, it was useless to keep up the old pretense that in their off-screen lives they were any different. It took a genuine leap of the imagination to identify in the twenties with the screen character of Valentino or Barrymore or Garbo or Gilbert, so exotic were the settings in which they appeared, so improbable the situations in which they found themselves, the dialogue the subtitles reported. It required no such leap to identify with Cagney or Gable or Spencer Tracy. Speech, very simply, meant that the movies had to be more realistic. This is in no way intended to imply that Hollywood's vision of reality was ever, by and large, a particularly truthful one. It is simply to say that, along the road to the inevitable happy ending, there came to be a greater emphasis on believability in everything, from the words actors spoke to the settings in which they appeared. More important, sound broke down the wall of silence which had previously separated star and audience. Somehow we came to stand less in awe of them, to feel, heaven help us, that they were our friends. At this point teen-agers began writing stars for advice on everything from body odor to their love lives.

What this meant to the star system is summed up simply in a quotation from a wise Frenchman named Gustave Le Bon: "The gods and men who have kept their prestige for long have never tolerated discussion. For the crowd to admire, it must be kept at a distance." The sound film appreciably narrowed that distance as did the kind of publicity that came with it. The result was that the role of the stars in our lives would never again be totally analogous with that of the gods. Stars retained some godlike attributes, but the opportunities for a sybaritic existence safe behind the walls of their estates and the walls of the improbable legends which had been created for them were now over. From this point it was but a short distance to a picture in the fan magazines of a star playing chef at a neighborhood cookout.

Sound also increased the number of stars. In silents it had been necessary merely to play one of the half dozen or so types around which nearly all movies were built. If you were a woman you were basically either a virgin or a vamp; if you were a male you were either a collar-ad type or a romantic in either the Valentino or Fairbanks tradition. There were, therefore, fairly rigid lines drawn between the film genres. Previously, there had been comedies, romances and adventure films, with an occasional contemporary melodrama thrown in. Now the lines between these categories began to blur and we had comedy-dramas and romantic adventures.

In addition, there was a sharp upturn in the number of films that focused on contemporary life. In short, stars were called upon to represent not just types, but people in an infinite variety. They had to speak, of course, where previously they had only to mime rather broadly some rather broad ideas. But there was more to their increased duties than that. They had to retain at least part of their old-time romantic appeal and yet, at the same time, be recognizable and believable (realistic) human beings. In the thirties that odd blend of reality and fantasy which the movies continue to offer us was mixed for the first time. A new kind of cinematic speech was developed, as Stanley Kauffman noted, a "tight-packed wisecrackese which *sounds* like life, but really is the twentieth-century American theater's equivalent of blank verse. . . . It is an American convention, an abstraction." As with the dialogue, so with the films; they looked a good bit like life, but they were not. Similarly the actors: they looked like real people, but of course, they were not; they remained movie stars.

So the star stopped being a mere type, a sort of incarnated mythic figure, as he had been, and it became fashionable to say that, instead, the stars played themselves. "Generally speaking, they do not," says Rod Steiger. "They play the image they have been successfully presenting over the years. It is not the person you find when you see them in private life. And in most cases, that is quite fortunate."

Says Richard Widmark: "Movie audiences fasten on to one aspect of the actor; they hold on to a piece of the personality for dear life, and then they decide what they want you to be. They think you're playing yourself. The truth is that the only person who can ever really play himself is a baby. . . . In each succeeding movie, you're virtually starting all over. The actor is tested again each time. If you're successful, you've been there, they've seen you, and they're measuring you against the time before."

Which brings us to the point of defining the modern movie star. The successful movie star continues to have certain magical abilities that are, to be sure, godlike. Through strength, agility and wit, he triumphs in situations where the ordinary mortal would fail or be defeated. But it is essential that through his manner—and mannerisms—he appear to be, at least up to the moment of his greatest trial, a recognizable human being. When he swings into his climactic action it must require no great effort for us to suspend disbelief as we watch him triumph over incredible odds. The identifying mannerisms—Bogart's lisping snarl, Cagney's rapid-fire diction, the sleepy roll of Brando's eye—all help us to identify with him in this moment, for all of us have such human attributes.

It is obviously for this reason that the most durable stars have been people who are not *perfectly* beautiful in appearance. Pretty boys and girls disappear quickly from the screen. Mere beauty is the simplest thing for Hollywood to find, and the ingenues and juveniles have always been the most easily interchangeable parts in the production machinery. The problem, in the usual Hollywood career, is to use those fleeting years of grace to develop some rough edges that will catch in the minds of audiences, thereby allowing the actor to develop a mature career. "Your personality," says Widmark, "is what the movie medium draws out and uses." The implication is that there must be something there for the camera to draw upon.

This means, of course, that it is irrelevant to apply the ordinary standards of acting to the movie performance. It is essential that the movie star appear to be, at least in the broad outlines of his performance, always the same. Personality always dominates the film and it is that which makes movies so soothing to jangled nerves—and, perhaps, prevents them from becoming high art. However hopeless things appear to be, we know this personality, and we know, too, that in crisis it will react in an all-too-familiar way, but a

way unknown to those who, in the screenplay, are plaguing it. Suspense is generated as we wait for the inevitable, that predictable explosion of personality which will carry all before it; the difference between a good film and a bad one lies in the amount of ingenuity used to work out the details leading up to this explosion.

There are, of course, dozens of other ways to make movies. It happens that this is the American way, the classic convention of a dramatic form that is peculiarly our own. To prefer other conventions is the privilege of the onlooker. But that is a matter of taste, hardly the occasion for a sermonette on the inadequacies of the convention as it has grown up here. What this means for the actor, very simply, is that he is engaged in a highly stylized form of art. This stylization imposes severe limitations on his work. His role is as predetermined, by the image he has created, more or less naturally out of the materials of his personality, as is the nature of man in Calvinist theology. He cannot escape this self which he has created on the screen.

In the classic drama of Greece the course of the tragedy is predetermined by the interaction of the laws of the gods and the single, tragic flaw of the hero. On the American screen the course of the action is predetermined by the limitations of the personalities involved. There is no formal body of law (unless you count the rules of the M.P.P.A. moral code) which the personality transgresses at his peril, but the rules for his behavior are nevertheless rigidly defined by a kind of common law based on past performance. Penalties for violators occur not during the course of the action on screen but outside of it, in the court of public opinion. The form of punishment for major violations is brutally primitive; it is ostracism from the community. Thus does the audience participate in a dim and ill-defined way in the dramatic lives of its screen heroes and heroines.

Movies are probably the only theatrical form in the cultural history of man in which the work itself (the individual film) is not an entity in itself but is only an incident in a larger drama—the total career of its stars. The form of the work is conditioned by works which have preceded it, and the current film will determine the nature of the one which will follow it.

Thus, the life of the screen star is a tangle of reality and fantasy. The roles he accepts will affect the nature of his private life, his reputation as a private individual will affect the nature of the roles he is offered. Some movie stars, if they are swashbucklers on the screen, may swashbuckle their way through life without fear of punishment. Errol Flynn, for instance, was a well-known ladies' man (sometimes under-age ladies at that). If anything, his screen career was advanced by public knowledge of this fact. The two images, real and fancied, happily coincided. Charles Chaplin, whose screen career consisted of the masterful playing of a highly stylized image of the common man, was, on the other hand, ruined in the eyes of the public by his numerous divorces, his minority political views and his involvement in a paternity suit. Reality could not be squared with the character the public desperately wanted him to be. Similarly, Ingrid Bergman, who acted with impressive candor and directness about her affair with director Roberto Rossellini, was the object of violent speeches on the floor of Congress and was ostracized for years by her public because she transgressed the rules established by her public personality, which projected a sort of rustic wholesomeness. At almost the same time, another screen star was publicly touring the continent in the company of an Eastern potentate-playboy. And although interest in their affair ran high, her transgression fitted neatly the sexy nature of her screen personality. There was no strong reaction to her affair.

All this leads to a simple conclusion: Movie stars are not basically actors, although many of them demonstrate mimetic gifts of a high order. They are, simply, empty vessels who indicate to us the kind of fantasies with which they and their superiors in the production hierarchy want us to fill them. If we respond to these hints, they will succeed. The superstars, the ones who seem to go on forever, are archetypes, answering the basic human needs for identification. Age cannot wither, custom cannot stale the pleasures they afford. Others are very much the products of special circumstances. They rise and fall in a brief span of time, answering a sudden socio-psychological need, then disappear almost as quickly as they appeared. In short, movie stars are objects of pure pleasure. And it is as such that they should be considered, not as actors or as artists.

There are difficulties involved in being such an object in our society. We have never been a nation inclined to take pleasure for pleasure's sake. We tend to look for social usefulness to justify our fun. Hence the insistence of stars that they are, indeed, actor-artists; hence, too, the contempt in which the star is often held by stage actors and by his fellow craftsmen in the industry, and the peculiarly ambivalent attitude of both critics and intelligent public toward the star. The simple folk simply love certain movie stars; and they go, a pleasurable tingle of anticipation buoying them on their journey, to see them as they expect to see them. If a role or an incident in the star's life disappoints them or alters their image of the actor, they merely find a new favorite. But

few intellectuals have the honesty to admit, as the admirable Robert Warshow did, "that I go to the movies for the same reason that the 'others' go: because I am attracted to Humphrey Bogart or Shelley Winters or Greta Garbo; because I require the absorbing immediacy of the screen; because in some way I take all that nonsense seriously." The average intelligent moviegoer is always trying to validate his attendance at the movies by some elaborate rationale. He and his fellows, in Paul Rosenberg's fine phrase, "have come not to bathe in the waters, but to register the degree of its pollution."

The burden of this book, very simply, is that by merely existing, movie stars fulfill whatever function they have in this world. It takes no moral position on the question of whether their existence—or, for that matter, the existence of movies as an institution—is "good" or "useful" in our society. My purpose is descriptive; my method is one which combines factual reporting about the lives of various film stars along with an analysis of what I think the essences they have projected have meant to us at various times. It is my hope that amateur sociologists, social historians and social psychologists among my readers will find some food for thought about the larger forces in our cultural history in the little descriptive and analytical pieces which follow. At the very least I hope everyone will enjoy the pictures which take up more space than the words in this book. Movie stars are really meant to be looked at, not talked about. If you have the eyes to see, you should be able to perceive what a star is, or was, all about, merely by looking.

In this connection I would like to offer a final analogy in the hope that it will get us off on the right foot. A movie star is not an artist, he is an art object. The performance one witnesses on the screen (and, for that matter, in his public life) is created by many hands—the star included. You cannot discuss this objectification of conscious and unconscious impulses as you would the work of a more conventional actor. The star's career is like a piece of sculpture—perhaps one of Alexander Calder's mobiles. If you like the piece of sculpture you will return to the museum on many occasions—on rainy afternoons, when you are feeling depressed or anxious or even elated—to seek a reestablishment, through it, of your connection with the world, your sense of continuity with it. It is the same with film stars. There are those democrats among us who can't see the use of either a piece of sculpture or a star. Neither is important since man could exist without them. Both are, however, realities of the general culture of our time. And both, in their ways, are creations in which we can see much and from which we can learn.

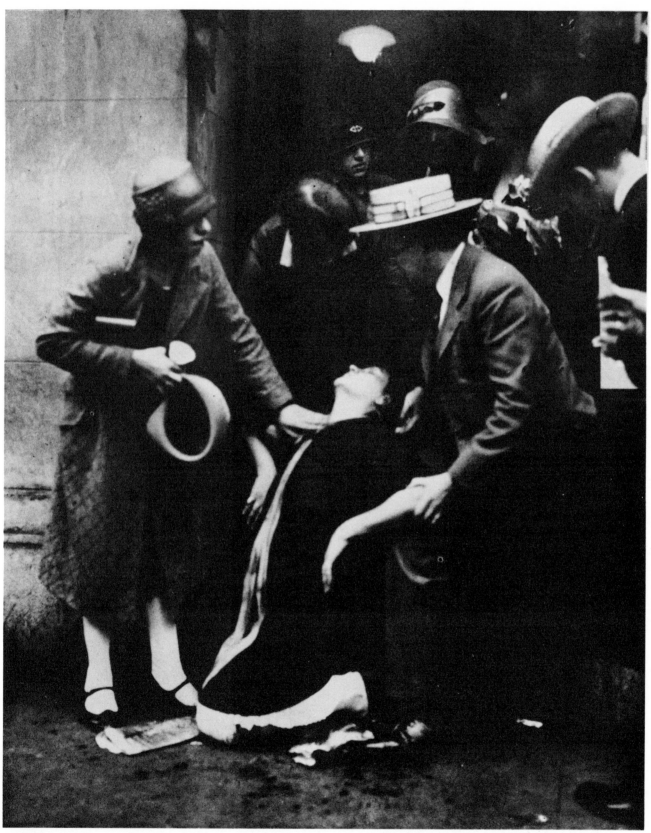

All passion spent. An anonymous fan, injured in the riotous rush on Frank Campbell's New York funeral home where Valentino lay in state, receives first aid. His death, in August, 1926 touched off an unparalleled frenzy in fandom. The hysterical behavior of his admirers has remained a symbol of all that is unhealthy in the relationship of star to public, though that relationship has been considerably modified over the years.

THE

PART ONE

PROTOTYPES

THE HISTORY OF AMERICAN MOVIES from 1907, when they took their first great leap toward economic power, to 1914, when the star system attained its first great flowering, cannot be told in terms of personalities—at least not in terms of star personalities. As we have already noted, there was no such thing until 1910, although a handful of people, like comedian John Bunny and an ersatz cowboy named Bronco Billy Anderson, were beginning, with no cooperation at all from the studios, to create an audience for their screen personalities. No, the real interest of these early, almost prehistoric, days lay in the realm of economics.

Thomas Edison had shown his first movie in 1896, and the history of American films is usually dated from that year, although the Lumières in France and the Lathams here both have excellent prior claim to the invention of movies, and several almost forgotten inventors have claims as good as Edison's. Indeed, it was not Edison at all, but one of his assistants, William Kennedy Dickson, who did most of the work on the new gadget. Be that as it may, Edison was in almost complete control of the business in its early stages. Whatever the other merits of his intelligence, Edison was not culturally very astute. He kept his camera crews cranking away, making stereopticon slides that moved, and very little else. At best, these efforts reached the level of crude newsreels, and when the novelty of "moving" pictures had worn off, the movies were in danger of death through intellectual malnutrition.

Two artists came to their rescue. The first was George Méliés, a magician who saw in movies the potential for the greatest trick of all. In the space of a few years at the turn of the century he devised most of the camera and editing tricks that still delight the eye today. Even more important, he took to arranging scenes in a simple sequence telling a simple story. He had a wonderful gift for fantasy and his early films are still delightful to see—and genuinely funny. An Edison cameraman, Edwin S. Porter, chanced on some of them and, because he had what others lacked—an eye to see—recognized the tremendous advance Méliés had made. Being an American, he was more interested in reality than fancy. So, when with Edison's blessing he set out to imitate Méliés, he turned his attention to the everyday world around him. The first American story film, *The Life of an American Fireman*, was assembled mainly from film clips, and it told very, very simply the story of a woman and child imperiled by flames and of their rescue by firemen. Technically, its great advance lay in the fact that Porter broke each separate scene down into individual shots. He even essayed a close-up—of an alarm box ringing. Very little attention was paid to the film, movies at this point having been relegated to the bottom of the bill at the less fashionable vaudeville houses. Porter was apparently undismayed; he went ahead with his second feature, and it made history. *The Great Train Robbery* was a Western, shot in New Jersey in 1903; the simple tale it told of frontier robbery and retribution, complete with a perfectly admirable chase, lifted movies out of the vaudeville houses and created a demand for more story films. Shortly thereafter, small capitalists began to rent little stores in poor neighborhoods and install folding chairs, projectors

and screens. The nickelodeon had arrived. Nearly all of them programed *The Great Train Robbery* first, then demanded more of the same. Other capitalists, only slightly larger, went into the business of satisfying them and, nickel by nickel, the business began to grow.

This was not totally pleasing to Mr. Edison. He had patents, and it seemed to him that these granted the exclusive right to make movies as well as to sell the equipment to shoot and project them. Suddenly hundreds of people were infringing on his rights, and profitably, too. By 1907 there were film rental exchanges in thirty-five key cities in America, and there were about eight thousand nickelodeons. The former brought a measure of stability to both the production and distribution ends of the business, while the latter were creating a steady, mass market for movies among the poorer classes. In 1907 Edison, despairing of winning all the suits he had launched for patent infringement, created the famous movie trust, which was designed to get the exhibitor coming and going. He had to pay a pegged rental fee for his films, which he had to show on equipment leased from the trust. The exhibitors, for the most part, responded very poorly to this attempt at coercion, and those producers not included in the trust went blithely ahead, making pictures, although many of them transferred operations to a sleepy suburb of Los Angeles known as Hollywood. This was sufficiently far from New York to make it difficult for the trust to trouble them, and sufficiently close to the Mexican border so that escape would be easy in the unlikely event that it became necessary. Also, the climate was good and you could shoot outdoors almost all year round. By 1914, even before the courts struck it down, the effect of the trust on the movie business had been almost completely mitigated.

Aesthetically speaking, the only thing the trust contributed to movie history was a place for D. W. Griffith to learn his craft. He came to Biograph—one of the trust studios—in 1909, part-time "serious" writer, part-time actor, and full-time Southern gentleman of the old school. He made hun-

dreds of one-reelers for Biograph, experimenting with camera, shots, lighting, editing, creating the basic style of the movie as we now know it. By the time he left Biograph, irritated by the limits it placed on his talents, he was ready to complete the transformation of the movie business. He gathered the remnants of his stock company, the actors who had as yet to receive billing and large salaries from Biograph, along with such key technicians as cameraman Billy Bitzer and in 1914 made *The Birth of a Nation,* a film weak in philosophy, but strong in cinematic technique. His reputation, high before the arrival of the first feature-length films from abroad. diminished it, now soared to new heights. The American companies had fought the introduction of features, but Griffith's smashing success now swept the industry into the production of long films—something for which Griffith had been fighting for years.

Films now became a major investment, and the days when a profitable one-reeler could be turned out in less than a week, on a budget of a couple of hundred dollars, were finished. Even the last holdouts, like Biograph, saw that the best insurance for these large investments were stars. Unfortunately for the holdouts, men like Carl Laemmle, William Fox and Adolph Zukor had sensed this much earlier and the older studios, which had become household names in the first ten years of the industry, found that their most potent players had been lured away. Most of them withered, and the new empires, from which all the current Hollywood studios are direct descendants, took their place. They were empires based on stars.

The first stars were, for the most part, players who went right on doing what they had been doing in their days of anonymity, only now with raised salaries and egos. Their vehicles were no longer as improvisational as the one-reelers had been, more attention was paid to accuracy and appropriateness of costume and scenery, and the scope of action and variety of locale were enormously increased. Only the basic character types of the people about whom the stories

*That "severe yet impassioned figure," William S. Hart,
indulges playful "Little Mary" on United Artists lot,
which she helped establish and where he fought for survival.*

revolved remained constant. There were villains and they were rarely stars (until, during World War I, Erich Von Stroheim emerged as "the man you love to hate"). There were heroes mainly of the jut-jawed, clean-limbed variety, (like J. Warren Kerrigan, Francis X. Bushman, Harold Lockwood, Carlyle Blackwood). There were, it seemed, dozens of youthfully beautiful heroines, whose principal characteristics were often epitomized by their screen names (like Arline Pretty, Louise Lovely). Each of them was, as one critic said of Lillian Gish, "a permanent lyric of jumpiness."

The early moguls—notably Zukor—were under the impression that one star was as good as the next, so long as the name had been properly sold; and many a Broadway name trekked west, seeking an easy fortune in movies. A few of them, like the Farnum brothers, did well. Most of them, however, proved rather too mature in appearance and manner for the tastes of their new audience, which tended to take a somewhat simplified view of things. Thespian reputations built on a talent for the then fashionable declamatory style of the stage meant little to it; beauty, the ability to communicate a sort of average attractiveness did. If the hero seemed to be a swell guy, the heroine a sweet child, they were taken to the collective bosom. The intimacy of the movie medium, the relative cultural naïveté of the audience defeated older, perhaps more serious, talents, and the first group of movie stars was drawn from the younger players.

Those who were merely pretty or handsome faded fairly quickly, their comeliness to be replaced by another group who would, in turn, be replaced by yet another youth movement when the first wrinkles appeared. Such temporary stars are an ongoing movie phenomenon which need not detain us long. Their only real interest is as a mirror of a decade's fads and fashions. But in that first group of stars, as is true in each generation of beautiful people, there were a few who were more than merely pretty. For them, physical attractiveness was merely the key which enabled them to unlock some

basic response in the vast majority of their audience. So basic was this appeal, so much of us—or, at least, of our longings—did they express, that they became the prototypes for most future stars.

In this chapter we consider two such people: Douglas Fairbanks, the perfect American hero; and Mary Pickford, a common-denominator sort of girl, the ideal wife, daughter, sister of a generation. Allowing for superficial variations based on changed tastes in style, dress and manner, Doug and Mary are still very much with us on the screen today. The same may be said of William S. Hart and Theda Bara, although their own careers were comparatively brief. Miss Bara was the movie industry's first try at a foreign temptress. They tried too hard, and poor Theda was laughed off the screen. But the foreign woman, more sensual, more worldly-wise than the typical American heroine, abides—exotic, temperamental, dangerous, but infinitely attractive. William S. Hart's demise may be blamed on his times. Temporarily, the romanticism of the 1920's, its insistent debunking of the old, rural values, forced him from the screen. But The Westerner, a sort of last Adam ranging a lost Eden, is too important a figure in American mythology to disappear completely. He returned, impersonated by others, in scripts that explored the type more deeply than did those of Hart, during our search for values in the 1930's. His type is still with us today, a more and more poignant reminder of what we lost when we uprooted ourselves from the land and decided to live lives of noisy desperation in a world growing more hectic every day. As for the Keystone Kops, they were the first great comedy stars, an ensemble of unparalleled virtuosity, creating nearly all that was great in screen comedy.

These, then, are our prototype screen personalities. A little of them survives in nearly every film made today, just as a little bit of Griffith's work survives in everything we see on the screen. They did not know it then, but they were creating, these early stars, the almost unchanging personality profile of the American film.

MR. SENNETT

The Kops and clowns, the ups and downs

"YOU KNOW," SAID THE LATE SNUB POLLARD, one of the original Keystone Kops, "I guess I've been bathed in no less than ten tons of very wet cement. I figured up once I'd caught about fourteen thousand pies in my puss and had been hit by six hundred automobiles and two trains. Once I was even kicked by a giraffe."

These hardships occurred in the pursuit of a most peculiar art, an art which flourished only briefly, then disappeared, done in by technology, pseudo-sophistication and, perhaps, a decline in the creative energy of the group which forged the unique, the incomparable style of silent screen comedy in the manic *atelier* of Mack Sennett.

The Keystone Kops in particular, Sennett's entire group in general, achieved stardom *en masse*. From time to time a particularly strong personality—a Chaplin, a Harry Langdon, a Keaton—would emerge from the gang and strike off on his own, having developed his trade in this school of hard knocks. But by and large the Kops and their quarries stand as anomalies in the history of stardom. A good many strange people have achieved stardom, but no group of this size— and nature—made it, either before or since. This is in character, for the Keystone group always stood a little outside the main stream of film history. There was really only one thing they could do—make Keystone comedies—and very few of them survived the coming of sound. Even at the height of their powers the kind of film they were making had about the same relationship to the rest of movie making as the work of S. J. Perelman has to the art of the novel. The same basic tools (camera and film, pen and paper) are used, but after that the similarity ends.

The Kops were the sole creation of Mack Sennett, an in-different actor who worked for Griffith at Biograph, graduated to scenario writing, then to the supervision of rube comedies. He paid generous tribute to Griffith as the man who "was my day school, my adult education program, my university," and indeed, his emphasis on movement in the comedies is certainly related to the theories of Griffith, as is his editing technique. But the source of Sennett's work

Ben Turpin suggests to some of his colleagues that they step to the rear of the car.

lies inexplicably deeper. It seems that all his life he regarded the policeman as one of God's more absurd creations. Probably it was the silly majesty the law attempts to maintain in the pursuit of minor offenders, its pitiful attempts at dignity in the face of man's obvious irrationality, which attracted Sennett to his great theme. In any case, he tapped a basic American feeling about policemen and allowed the nation to vent its dislike of regulations in gales of laughter. Law is such a sad thing, trying as it does to capture the basic absurdity of human behavior and pen it behind walls of rationally conceived rules. Our instinctive knowledge of the hopelessness of the task is what triggers our laughter at a Sennett comedy.

In this we are aided by the Kops themselves. We think of Sisyphus, toiling to push his rock up the hill, fully aware that, at the moment of triumph, the gods will send it tumbling back to the ground below. The Kops seemed to sense the futility of their activities, but the game itself was the fun, and their hopelessly befuddled chase after the miscreant, typically in a decrepit flivver from which their blue-clad arms and legs protruded in wild tangles, their faces meanwhile maintaining a stolid dignity that defied us to comment upon the mess they were making, was something into which you could read a dozen meanings. Certainly, it is not too pretentious to say that the Kops, who in Agee's phrase, "zipped and caromed about the pristine world of the screen as jazzily as a convention of water bugs," made a valid comment on all who pursue goals with too much zeal and not enough thought about ultimate values.

Beyond all this, there was the beautifully simple cinematic style in which these splendid fellows went through their paces. Sennett believed speed and grotesquery were the basis of comedy. Few Sennett gags took more than ten seconds of screen time from initial statement, through elaboration, to culmination. Ideally the next gag was built off the first and sight gag followed sight gag in dizzying succession. Even when he was supervising the entire product of his busy studio and directing very little, he reviewed every scene shot, the creakings of his projection-room rocker an index to his responses. He always called for more speed. As to his liking for the grotesque, one need only look at the faces and figures of the actors he employed. They were parodies of the human form, and that made their parodies of poor man's attempts to cope with the essentially unmanageable modern world even more delicious. The backgrounds against which they moved, the wasteland of southern California when it was a subdivider's paradise, with only the skeleton of the megalopolis to come sketched in, enhanced the mood of dreamlike realism in Sennett's films. Finally, the girls, really quite lovely, and the first direct screen statement of the pleasures inherent in the female form were a perfect touch. The bathing beauties represented a healthy kidding of our sexual preoccupations. They were neither simpering nor blatant in manner. They simply existed, delightful, not quite bright, ideal foils for the cavorting grotesques around them.

The Sennett star faded quickly after the coming of sound. His most talented mimes had already left him, and then tastes changed, and the verbal gag replaced the visual one in films. Sennett ended his days broke and—like so many movie pioneers—almost forgotten by the industry he helped create. Most of the artists who followed his traditions and work, were also ruined by sound. It is only now—too late—that we see in the artless art of Mack Sennett more real worth than in all but a handful of the more grandiose productions of his contemporaries. He is one of the few who made genuine folk art while working in the mass media.

The bathing beauties seem to be under the impression they work for Isadora Duncan instead of Mack Sennett (above).

WILLIAM S. HART
The first American hero

"... THERE WAS WILLIAM S. HART with both guns blazing and his long, horse face and his long, hard lip, and the great country rode away behind him as wide as the world." So the first great Man of the West appeared to a small boy named James Agee, opening for him and his generation a vision of spaciousness and freedom that had once been an integral part of the American dream, but which was now, in a rapidly urbanizing nation, disappearing.

As the land was changing, so were the people, and if the West seemed like a lost Eden, Hart seemed to be the last Adam. Neither God nor man dictated to him. He appeared to have arrived on the side of goodness through reason and free choice. Characteristically, he appeared out of nowhere, giving no hint about either background or motivation, suggesting only that in his past lay an unnamed evil which he had to expiate.

The fact that he portrayed a good guy was more important to the moralistic Hart than it was to his audience. His rectitude provided an acceptable sanction for his real business, which was to "defend the purity of his own image—in fact his honor." It was this defense of the self, in a world which increasingly forces the individual to compromise with his idealized self-image, that was the root of Hart's popularity, and, for that matter, the popularity of all his successors in the role of the great American archetype.

In addition, Hart demonstrated ways and means by which the individual could defend his self-image against intrusion. They were manly ways, having nothing to do with keeping your nose clean and waiting for the boss to notice you. "The essence of the hero," Parker Tyler notes, "may be defined as a super sort of professionalism. All men desiring greatness

Hart established the convention that the Western hero loved his horse more than his heroine. He was capable of sensuality, but not of real love.

Face of a Hero: the difference between
pleasure and disgust was no
more than the twitch of a tiny muscle.

The defense of innocence: After the rescue, "he made a bashful face at a girl and his horse raised its upper lip and everybody laughed."

Hart on location: "I was content. I was surrounded by no greedy grafters, no . . . slimy creatures—just dogs, horses, sheep, goats, bulls, mules, burros and . . . men.

in the public eye . . . undergo a difficult discipline and the acquisition of an elaborate system of knowledge." Hart's Westerner had done so; he rode and shot with preternatural skill, had available to him the most obscure bits of outdoor know-how, insuring his triumph in difficult situations. He was, in short, that most admired American phenomenon, the Old Pro, so sure in his hard-won skills that his mere presence was a comfort.

Hart himself seems to have been unaware of the depths he had touched in the nation's unconscious. A rather average stage actor who had spent most of his boyhood in the West, he had been appalled by the lack of realism in the early Westerns, had begged his friend the producer Thomas Ince for a chance to do honest films about the West. Ince, thinking that the genre's popularity was finished, had only grudgingly given Hart his chance. His first, a stark little item called *The Bargain,* was a surprise hit, and Ince had to bring Hart back to Hollywood from New York, whither he had retreated, convinced that there would be no more Westerns suitable for him. Ince, who had merged with Griffith and Sennett to form Triangle, exploited Hart shamelessly, keep-

ing his salary low while his popularity leaped upward. Whenever Hart complained, the producer played on the actor's strong and simple sense of loyalty to keep him in line, preventing him from capitalizing on his popularity until it had passed its peak.

Triangle was finally absorbed by Paramount, and Hart received an excellent contract, but he was soon dropped, and that studio, then in control of the strongest theater chain in the nation, kept his subsequent independent productions out of the best houses. Commercially, they were probably right. Hart's attention was too firmly fixed on such surface matters as realism of setting and simplicity of moral. In the twenties, when the traditional morality of rural America, on which Hart had based his work, was in retreat from the disorderly assaults of the younger generation, and when the mass audience was more interested in romance than in reality, he was woefully out of step. He turned down *The Covered Wagon,* a great comeback opportunity, because it lacked realism, and retired to his ranch. He refused to allow development of its oil resources, not wanting his view to be spoiled by derricks.

"These hills were mine, and had been mine since my birth."
—WILLIAM S. HART

THEDA BARA

The dark lady of the publicity stills.

A vamp there was

THIS WAS THE LEGEND they concocted for Theda Bara: She was born in the Sahara, love child of a French artist and his Arab paramour. Her name was an anagram for "Arab Death." She had a seer's power, habitually wore indigo to accentuate the deathly pallor of her skin, surrounded herself with the symbols of death—mummy cases, ravens, skulls. To love her was to die or, at the very least, to be unmanned.

Theodosia Goodman, the "circumspect and demure" daughter of a Cincinnati tailor did her best to live the legend and, for a time, she appalled the genteel, outraged the moral, amused the cynical and, in general, packed 'em in. It was her refreshing exoticism, in the midst of so many golden-haired virgins, that attracted. It was her publicity that ruined her. The wish for death and the will to love may indeed spring from the same libidinal source, but it is unwise to insist on the point; it makes people very nervous indeed. Audiences began to titter uncomfortably, then to laugh uproariously and with a great sense of relief. Miss Bara's career was over. What she established, however, the lure of the exotic, the absolutely un-American woman, had a peculiar immortality.

A Fool There Was, *the film that launched Theda Bara in 1914.*

The virgin dynamo

Small animals were a customary Pickford prop, as
they are for a latter-day child-woman named Brigitte Bardot.

MARY PICKFORD

"ALTHOUGH THEATERS, STUDIOS and exchanges in 1917-18
represented investments of several millions of dollars and
gave employment to a hundred thousand people, Mary Pickford remained the industry's most valuable asset. Woman's
place in business has grown enormously in importance in the
last three decades, but Mary Pickford is the only member of
her sex who ever became the focal point of an entire industry. Her position was unique; probably no man or woman
will ever again win so extensive a following." So wrote
Benjamin Hampton in his *History of the Movies*, and he did
not exaggerate. Little Mary's mere presence in the industry
was a strong defense against reformers, who had raised a hue
and cry against movies almost as soon as they were born.
When the charge that movies corrupted youth was raised,
the industry merely pointed to Miss Pickford, and reminded
critics of the lesson which her standard plot (and her
career) taught.

She was a virgin in almost constant peril. Yet she was both
plucky and optimistic, even surprisingly resourceful in de-
feating the heavily armed enemies who surrounded her.
As Bill Hart asserted man's right to freedom, so Mary

A big moment from Little Lord Fauntleroy. *At the
time Miss Pickford was 29 years old.*

*Little Mary working under the direction of D. W.
Griffith. The picture is* The New York Hat *(1912).*

Pickford asserted woman's right to remain inviolate. Like Hart, she was satisfyingly victorious in defense of both the immediate symbol and that larger abstraction, personal integrity. Later critics have suggested that her appeal was not altogether based on purity, that there were subtle suggestions of the nymphet about her—-but the evidence is slim and, even at this late date, somehow shocking.

Little Mary was born Gladys Smith in Toronto. Both the tenacity and the shrewdness which were part of her screen character were undoubtedly borrowed from life. Her mother was her first—and most passionate—admirer, as well as the guiding genius behind her career. Gladys played her first role in a Toronto stock company at five; at twelve she was playing leads; in her teens she was touring; when she was seventeen she got her first Broadway part from David Belasco, who also gave her the name under which she would become America's Sweetheart. When the play closed in May 1910, she turned up at the Biograph studio looking for work.

David Wark Griffith took just one day to get her before a camera—in *The Violin Maker of Cremona.* She was his type, a romantic's golden vision of the innocence of youth. She started at twenty-five dollars a working day, rose to a guaranteed hundred dollars a week, was lured to Carl Laemmle's IMP concern for a slight raise and more artistic freedom than she had under the iron ego of Griffith. She went back to the stage in 1913, in Belasco's *The Good Little Devil,* and never returned to living theater again. The part qualified her for a contract with Audolph Zukor's Famous Players, which prom-

ised the players presentation "in famous plays." That policy didn't work out; but Mary Pickford did. Within a few years Zukor was paying her $500,000 a year, and she was worth it. In those days of block booking you could force an exhibitor to swallow a lot of indifferent pills by dangling before him the prospect of playing the new Pickford. In due course she left Paramount (Famous Players under another name) to form her own company, then went on with her new husband, Douglas Fairbanks, to form United Artists.

He had a natural gift for production, she had learned well the financial lessons her mother had taught her—and the tenacity. "She never stopped listening and learning," Griffith said. "She was determined to learn everything she could about the business." She learned so well that, without ever raising her voice, she acquired a fortune her old mentor, Griffith, who never did understand money, must have envied in his pitiful last years. "It often took longer to make one of Mary's contracts than it did to make one of Mary's pictures," Samuel Goldwyn once observed.

Ambitious, clever, never anything but the gracious, modest "glad girl" of her publicity, she was forever the woman every mother wanted for a daughter, every man for a sister. And a sore trial for free spirits and sophisticates. Mabel Normand, whose career was ruined by scandal, summed up their point of view one time when an interviewer asked her what her hobby was. "Say anything you like," she replied, "but don't say I like to work. That sounds too much like Mary Pickford, that prissy bitch."

34

The Taming of the Shrew *(1929) was Doug and Mary's first sound film and carried an immortal credit line:*
"By William Shakespeare. Additional Dialogue by Samuel Tayl

The Three Musketeers *(1921). The Americano has become the high-born savior of the people.*

IT TAKES AN URBAN CULTURE to produce a Douglas Fairbanks and, in truth, he was our first urbane movie hero. The "difficult discipline" he underwent and the "elaborate system of knowledge" he acquired to lay claim to our admiring attention, were utterly different from those of The Westerner. Fairbanks' skills were acquired not through communion with nature, but in the artificial atmosphere of the gymnasium. Similarly, his manner. Not for him the granitic countenance, the leisurely pace, the slowness of emotion which belong to the man attuned to nature's rhythm. Instead, he was quick, breezy, cheerfully optimistic, shallowly bright—a city man, a man whose business was business. He was, both on and off screen, an indoors man at a time when America was becoming an indoors nation. On the screen he proved to his audience that there need be nothing unmanly about its new way of life, that, whatever its critics might say, decent values could continue to exist, even flourish, in the new environment. Indeed, he implied that they could be adorned with a new grace and wit and style.

"At a difficult time in American history," Alistair Cooke writes, "Douglas Fairbanks appeared to know all the answers and knew them without pretending to be anything more than 'an all around chap, just a regular American.'" How comforting this was to a nation standing on the brink of a war in which it was clear that for the first time the courage of the new America would be tested in the ancient manner—trial by combat.

We tend to remember Fairbanks in terms of the romantic costume epics he produced for himself in the twenties. In war's aftermath Fairbanks, the canny showman, was among the first to sense the shift in taste from the everyday settings and situations of the flickers' early days toward highly romanticized material. Taking advantage of this, he leaped with his customary easy grace backward in time to distant places, but however he costumed himself he remained very much the same "Doug" he had always been. This personality was created in a single year, 1916, when he made eleven films—more than a quarter of his total output—on the Triangle lot. There Fairbanks, an irrepressible prankster, and an equally irrepressible gymnast, was encouraged to set his own pace, work out his own athletic improvisations on basically simple scripts. If, as some have suggested, the basic concern of Americans is not with end product but with process, then it was at the moment of these improvisations that Fairbanks achieved real greatness in our eyes. It was not important where or why Doug was going; what was important was *how* he went. Man is great, said Emerson, "not in his goals but in his transitions." Fairbanks, even in his late, mannered work, was the greatest maker of transitions in screen history.

DOUGLAS FAIRBANKS
The new American

Fairbanks, the new American hero, leads the cheers at a Liberty Loan rally in Wall Street, 1918.

The Thief of Bagdad (1924). More swagger, less naturalness now, but still recognizably Doug.

THE

PART TWO

TWENTIES

SOMEHOW, THE MOVIES BECAME socially acceptable between 1910 and 1920. Maybe the industry's wholehearted support of the war effort, in which it became the government's chief domestic propaganda arm, turned the tide in its favor. Maybe a new emphasis on creature comforts in theaters brought the middle classes in. Maybe it was the prestige which films of feature length seemed to create automatically. Or maybe it was simply that the lure of the medium could no longer be denied, no matter how hard you tried to maintain your respectability. Certainly, the clear appeal of stars like Hart, Pickford, Fairbanks and Chaplin helped mightily to erase lingering doubts about the moral correctness of "wasting time" at the movies. At any rate, the movies' battle for general acceptance by a larger group than the nickelodeon set was won.

But the life of commerce is never an easy one, and as soon as this plateau was reached, new demands were made upon the medium. The principal effect of World War I on the American mind was the creation of a revulsion against reality. We had entered the war with such high hopes— the world was to be saved for democracy, we were at last to assert the greatness of our democratic ideals on a cynical and materialistic world. Somewhere in France all the fine phrases turned to mud and those of our youth who returned from the ordeal found, in Scott Fitzgerald's perfect phrase, "all gods dead, all wars fought, all faiths in man shaken." It is probably not too much to say that these young men loathed the world and loathed themselves for having been duped by it. They wanted very much to forget all the things

most people regarded as important.

By default, the political affairs of the nation were placed in the hands of the most banal hacks in the history of the Republic. More serious minds turned to art as an escape from day-to-day reality, and never in America has there been such a creative ferment as occurred in the years between 1919 and 1929. But most people—including the older generation, who quickly caught the youngsters' mood —just decided to make money (which was easy) and to have fun (which was harder).

Since movies were certainly not an art form at the time and since they were clearly designed to entertain, rather than to enlighten, they followed the dictates of the great audience. They provided the nation with more escapes than Harry Houdini. "The Old Gang," that steadfast group of rustic moralists, fighting desperately to preserve what they conceived to be the American Way of Life, but what was in reality merely an irrelevant set of manners, quickly zeroed in on the movies as a prime cause of all the moral ills then afflicting the nation. When a number of Hollywood stars were caught in a series of scandals, the industry, which had previously ignored the cries from the hinterlands, hastily created the Hays office to police the content of films and, more importantly, the morals of the stars. It performed lackadaisically until 1933, when another wave of outrage forced the creation of The Code (*all rise*), a set of rules explicitly setting forth the things from which the camera must avert its eyes. During the twenties, the Hays office had been a sop to the outraged, a public-relations device, rather than a truly effective police agency.

There was nothing very serious to police in any case. Joseph Wood Krutch declared that "the inanities blessed by Mr. Hays are more genuinely corrupting than any pornography," and it is certainly true that the movies of the Jazz Age were more inane than they were dirty. The industry summed up its aims with great clarity in the course of its campaign urging Americans to "Go to a motion picture . . . and let yourself go." "Before you know it you are *living* the story—laughing, loving, hating, struggling, winning! All the adventure, all the romance, all the excitement you lack in your daily life are in—Pictures. They take you completely out of yourself into a wonderful new world . . . Out of the cage of everyday existence! If only for an afternoon or evening—escape!"

There is little point in analyzing the content of movies during the Dizzy Decade. The average film was merely a blend of ingredients designed to melt in your mind, a sort of primitive tranquilizer. There were all kinds of films attempting this task. There were sex comedies, revolving around infidelity and its wages, which Cecil B. DeMille turned out, usually featuring an obligatory bathtub sequence. There were the flapper films, dealing with the way youth was carrying on. There were the Graustarkian romances, all about the loves of royalty for commoners. There were, as objections to these forms mounted, Biblical epics which wrapped the cloak of Christian message around that most ancient of commodities, sex. There was, in time, an invasion of German and German-influenced craftsmen who came a curious cropper when they attempted to turn out the standard Hollywood product using expressionistic techniques, then all the rage on the Continent. Finally, there were the costume dramas and period pieces, pioneered by Fairbanks, and brought to their finest, most absurd flowering by Rudolph Valentino.

The high priestess of the new exoticism was Elinor Glyn, discoverer of "It" (meaning sex appeal and applied chiefly to a charming little flapper named Clara Bow), author of *Three Weeks* (first of the Graustarkian tales) and chief industry spokesman for romance. "I wanted to stir up in the cold hearts of the thousands of little, fluffy, gold-digging American girls a desire for greater joys in life than are to be found in candy boxes and car rides and fur coats," she declared, "a desire to be loved as European women are loved; and, as a result, a desire to give as well as to receive."

America was, at the time, in full-scale revolt against the old sexual standards and, as Malcolm Cowley noted, was declaiming against "American grossness and American puritanism in one breath and as if they were one and the same thing." The movies, with their emphasis on the pleasures of love in other climates, certainly made a strong statement against puritanism. The trouble was that the message was heavily tainted with grossness.

As for the stars themselves, their off-screen lives were expected to bear further witness against the drabness of ordinary American life. No less than three reigning female stars married minor European titles. Another toured Europe accompanied by a menagerie including a Russian wolfhound, a German dachshund, an English pointer, an Irish setter, and a St. Bernard. A minor comic who died broke had every door in his home equipped with solid-gold doorknobs. A leading man zipped around town in a low-slung, robin's-egg-blue car the horn of which played "Yankee Doodle Dandy." Valentino's home, Falcon's Lair, had a canary-and-black bedroom and a living room with blackmarble floor and cerise hangings. The radiator cap of his car sported a carefully worked cobra design.

It was all shocking and delicious—the parties, the love affairs, the occasional trouble in paradise. For, truly, the stars of the twenties were gods and everyone—everyone, that is, but the Old Gang—would have been terribly disappointed had they lived like ordinary mortals. Indeed, today certain theorists of the cinema, alarmed at the dreariness which has afflicted post-television Hollywood, have been urging a return to the bad old days. The notion is that people cannot get very excited about personalities who are publicized as just ordinary guys and gals. What are needed are stars who keep their distance, who emerge in public not to prove that they are just like everyone else but who demonstrate that they are utterly, and contempuously, different from you and me. Sound films, thirty years of leveling publicity and the new American social consensus formed in the 1930's prohibit that. And anyway, we have built new identifications with the stars. But there was a beautiful simplicity about our relationship to them in the twenties, not to mention a refreshing lack of subtleties for the social historian to comprehend.

Indeed, as one looks back upon the life of Hollywood in the twenties, from a distance of almost forty years, in a time when our moral outrage has shifted from the sybaritic stars to Madison Avenue, the television industry and the Hidden Persuaders, one is struck by the almost childlike innocence which underlay the old Hollywood public morality. There was a naïveté in its pretensions, a glorious unconcern about a future that would never arrive, which is quite touching. At least on the surface. What was going on

*The lady and the lion. Greta Garbo, symbol of
stardom, poses for a nervous publicity shot with Metro-
Goldwyn-Mayer's perfect symbol of the industry's
arrogance, pretension and, perhaps, lack of humanity.*

behind the scenes of the cinema was less appealing, for it was nothing less than the ruination of a potentially great art form.

At the end of World War I, motion pictures had not yet chosen the direction which they would take. A handful of artists had, by that time, created a number of primitive but genuine works of art. In them, as one views them now in the basement screening room of the Museum of Modern Art, one seems to detect what may have been the beginnings of an art form that was both popular and satisfying by higher artistic standards—rather like the plays of Marlowe, necessary precursors of Shakespeare. The trouble with movies is that a Shakespeare never arrived or, if he did, he was never allowed to develop his talents. The comedians, who did the most completely satisfying work of the period, stood outside the main line of commercial development in the industry and were mostly unappreciated by aestheticians until our own time. The immense talents of D. W. Griffith and Erich Von Stroheim could not be fitted into the developing commercial patterns and they were shunted to one side, various excuses, mostly economic, being offered for their ostracism. New and genuine talent from abroad, men like Victor Seastrom, Ernst Lubitsch, Mauritz Stiller, were either bent to the commercial exigencies or compelled to leave in disgust. Home-grown talent like John Ford and King Vidor created isolated masterpieces and developed to a high degree the art of aesthetic survival through trickery. The business of "slipping things by" front office and censors—a nasty little game fostered in all the mass media—flourished, giving sustenance to its inevitable and enervating parasite, cynicism.

All Hollywood could see were the forty million customers streaming into theaters every week to watch the stars go through their formula paces. Business on this scale surely caused the minds of the small, small businessmen, so lately removed from the nickelodeon days, to boggle. As for the banking interests who were, in the era of wild expansion, making greater and greater investments in movies, they thought they had bought into so many steel mills and were interested only in steady, profitable production.

As public relations devices, the studios occasionally turned out "art" films, but these were always literary rather than cinematic in artistic heritage; only the craftsmen of the industry sensed the true, and unique, nature of the medium's potential, but they had little to say about what was to be made. In the end, when the formula began to fail, after World War II, lack of vision received its true reward. In the meantime, there were the stars, and by them the industry set its erratic course. The trip was wonderful. What matter if no one knew the ultimate destination.

VALENTINO
The new romantic

It may be, after all these years, that we should readmit Rudolph Valentino to the human race. He was a man inordinately ill-served by everyone—the public, the press, the people who created and marketed his films, himself. His chief crime, in which all of these forces participated, was against the standard American concept of ideal manhood. He was too graceful and too beautiful—that was clear— but worse than that, he seemed weak. His weakness was merely sensed, sensed and commented upon by the American male, who did not like him, sensed and not admitted by the women, who did like him.

In the still-lingering afterglow of the hysteria he generated, he has become a kind of comic symbol of the excesses of his time and, indeed, there was much that was extremely funny about Valentino. There were, to begin with, the absurdly exotic settings in which his screen character was generally placed, not to mention the ludicrous costumes and *décor* with which they were freighted. But more important was the gap between the style he was forced to adopt in these films and the style that might have been natural to this rather shy and passive personality. The result was a terrible strain on him, and it is largely this strain which has been captured in the still photographs which are this generation's chief link with him. Adolph Zukor, who employed The Sheik, wrote that his acting "was largely confined to protruding his large, almost occult, eyes until vast areas of white were visible, drawing back the lips of his wide, sensuous mouth to bare his gleaming teeth, and flaring his nostrils." In other words, to indicate the outbursts of a smoldering flame that did not, in fact, exist, Valentino resorted to heroic Thespian exertions, defying all the laws of successful screen performance. The miracle is that he triumphed despite this nonsense.

For this triumph he could thank the sensibilities of the women, who detected beneath the fakery, the real Valentino. If you are not distracted by his wildly flailing attempts to indicate a quality quite beyond him, you can still detect this essential Valentino at odd moments in his films. There is, to begin with, the softness of his mouth when he forgets to set it in a hard, determined line, when he is not forcing it to leer. There is, in addition, the withdrawn sadness of his eyes in their unpopped condition. Finally, and most im-

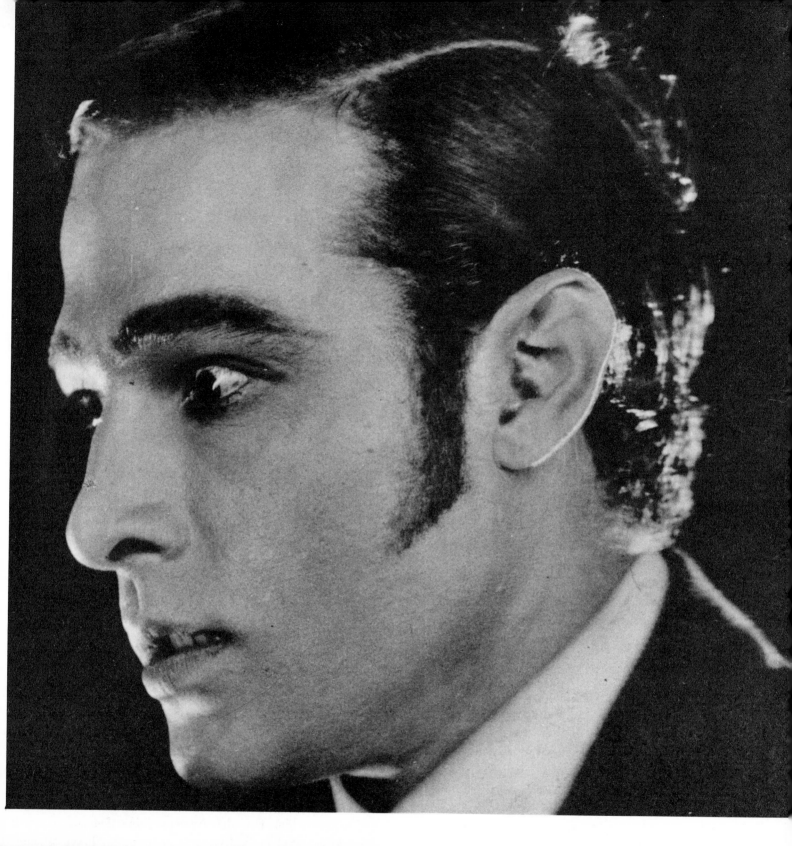

Valentino's build was anything but that of
"a pink powder puff." He was, however, a bit
of a fop; and the American male, outraged at his
effect on women, distrustful of his boudoir grace,
was not in a mood to choose his adjectives carefully. He was on stronger ground questioning
the sincerity of the passion Valentino projected.
The popping of the eyes (above) was one of his
habitual—and less successful—ways of communi-
cating something foreign to his rather passive
nature. He was much more comfortable playing it
straight (left) in Moran of the Lady Letty.

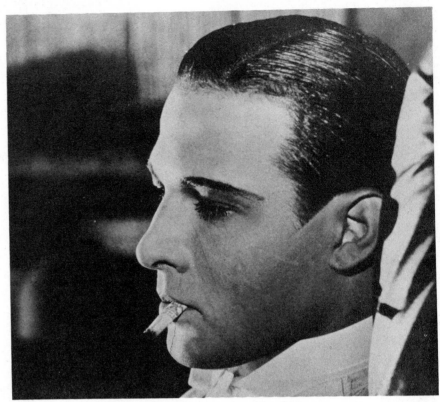

In The Sainted Devil *he managed an unwonted hardness.*

portant, there is the insinuating gracefulness of his movements when they are unencumbered by period costumes. It is not the grace of an athlete—it is quite un-Fairbanksian— it is the grace of, frankly, a seducer, perhaps even a gigolo. It is grace directed toward a single end—the smooth transfer of a woman from an upright to a reclining position. To waste such grace on a high jump or a pole vault would have been madness. To use it as he did was an insult to all the Anglo-Saxon traditions of male-female relations, refreshing to women, despicable to men. He was, in short, that infinitely attractive thing—a boy in man's clothing and a boy, what's more, with an obvious talent for sensuality, a talent which any woman might wish first to test and then to develop to a man's full-scale sexuality.

There has never been a movie star in whose presence women more wanted to be, no star they more wanted to touch. There seemed to spring in his fans an eternal hope that one of them would awaken the real forces that slumbered (as they thought) within him. They could see the strain which posing as a man of action caused him, they knew the gap between the pretenses his scenarios forced upon him and the real Valentino, and all of them thought they just might be the woman—if only he would just notice —through whom he could bridge the gap.

Undoubtedly they sensed the truth about the real man, that he was fatally attracted to women stronger than he was.

The one he chose as his wife very nearly succeeded in wrecking his career before his sudden death in 1926 ended it. She was a Salt Lake City girl named Winifred Shaunessy, stepdaughter of cosmetician Richard Hudnut. She was a designer and actress and in pursuit of these professions chose the cognomen Natacha Rambova. She began supervising Valentino's pictures and she emphasized the softness of his character, putting him into foppish items like *Monsieur Beaucaire*, presenting him with a slave bracelet that he wore to the great derision of the masculine American.

It was at this point that the Chicago *Tribune* called him a "pink powder puff" and suggested that he was setting a terrible example for American youth. Even the women began to desert him. For what Natacha didn't realize was that it was essential for Valentino to continue his brave attempts at strongly masculine behavior in his films. They served to remind his audience that there was a man within, a man waiting for release through love. The obligatory moment in his films where he threatened to—and sometimes actually did—take his heroine by force was, for his fans, a moment of high deliciousness. Beneath his demands, they sensed his gentleness. Once he had broken down resistance by its use they knew he would be gentle and kindly, a perfect lover. Without the tension between this fraudulent force and this real gentleness, Valentino was just a pretty profile, and that was what Natacha was reducing him to before they separated

It was pictures like this which ruined Valentino.

and he began his much publicized affair with Pola Negri.

Valentino himself sensed the discrepancy between his screen self and his real self, and as false film followed false film he complained, "I am beginning to look more and more like my miserable imitators." Many of them were indeed better at playing the Valentino character than was Valentino. Perhaps he so willingly followed Natacha's suggestions because he could no longer bear his pretense. He was, in any case, neither a stupid nor an insensitive man—despite the counterlegend his detractors created in the attempt to debunk him. He came from a relatively prosperous and educated provincial Italian family. He had a diploma from a college of landscape architecture, and he had come to America not as an immigrant seeking relief from oppression, but out of curiosity. He was a natural dancer, danced for pleasure in the hours after work as a gardener, then turned professional, taking over from Clifton Webb as Bonnie Glass's partner, touring with her until the act broke up in Los Angeles, where he found work as a minor movie player. Screen writer June Mathis sensed his appeal and brought him to Rex Ingram, who took a big chance by putting him into his arty super-production, *The Four Horsemen of the Apocalypse* at Metro, which, with notable lack of foresight, signed him only for that picture. Zukor picked him up before Metro quite realized what it had. The first film was a solid hit; *The Sheik,* made for Paramount, was a sensation, and the mold was cast.

You could not say that Valentino was an intellectual, but he did have a natural sensitivity, which was his undoing. Lacking the strength to assert himself, even to be cynical, he buried his resentments inside himself, devoted himself with a surprisingly professional attitude to trying, somehow, to make himself believable. Of his physical strength he was more sure, but it was not enough, especially when the attacks on his masculinity reached their late heights. Some of his personal idiosyncrasies, his foppish dress, the womanish quality of his temper, served his enemies better than they did Valentino. More and more, toward the end, he talked of the tragic heroes he wanted to play—especially Pirandello's men in search of identity. "A man should control his life," he said once, "mine is controlling me. I don't like it." The screen role he loved best was the one in *The Four Horsemen.* "Julio was a man who allowed his weakness to dictate his circumstances—myself," he once said. His death, creating the awesome outburst of madness which marred his memory irrevocably was caused by a perforated ulcer, that classic affliction of a man in debt to circumstance and unable to live with the debt.

Valentino as women saw him. The film is The Conquering Power.

Valentino as he saw himself. "A man should control his life," he said. "Mine is controlling me." Searching for identity himself, he wanted to play a Pirandello hero.

The Gilded Cage *was vintage Swanson, the star at top power.*

The rivals
SWANSON

Cecil B. DeMille first noticed Gloria Swanson leaning against a door while some of Mack Sennett's clowns gamboled by. At the moment she was just another girl who, for no good reason, thought she ought to be a movie star; a tiny, flat-chested, former ribbon clerk with the twang of the Middle West ringing loud and clear in her voice. DeMille thought there was a certain air of authority about her and guessed that she might be taught to project it on the screen. He swathed her in some of the damnedest costumes in Hollywood history, gave her a cigarette holder with which to gesture imperiously and had her hair redone in an outlandish manner which other ribbon clerks were led to think

"Gloria Swanson's greatest achievement is her own face in repose," said one magazine.

of as sophisticated. Then, in 1919, he popped her into the string of glittery films about upper-class infidelity he was making and told her to act the way she now looked. She should have failed, but she did not—perhaps because all her life she had been imagining how she would behave in just such situations as DeMille now placed her.

She was something new in movie stars, ruthless, arrogant, willful and therefore a challenge to every male who thought he was man enough to tame the tiger, a being for every little kitten to try to emulate. No one really loved the lady, but nearly everyone was awed by her.

There came a time when Adolph Zukor was willing to

pay her a million dollars a year to keep her under contract. She refused; having become imbued with art, she took to producing her own films at United Artists, and her stardom burned less bright. Meantime, by assertion of divine right, she ruled Hollywood, the very model of the movie queen. There were those who could not quite forget the little girl who had been part of the first wave of adolescent immigrants to fantasy land. But so completely did she transform herself, basing her new role on the ones she had played on the screen, that only one person, Pola Negri, dared challenge Gloria Swanson's supremacy—and she failed.

The rivals NEGRI

Pola Negri, before Hollywood (left) *in the German film* Sumurun, *and after. "I consider my work great, as I am a great artist."*

POLA NEGRI'S EARLY LIFE was as exotic as Gloria Swanson's was plain. She was a genuine gypsy, whose father had somehow become involved in Poland's fight for independence from Russia and was exiled to Siberia as a result. After his death there, Pola attended the Imperial Ballet School, achieved theatrical success in Warsaw, and stardom in Berlin under Max Reinhardt. Along the way she married and discarded a count whose chief contribution to her life was a title which she flaunted at every opportunity.

Success in an aptly titled Lubitsch epic, *Gypsy Blood*, brought her to the Paramount lot as a sort of modified vamp. There she immediately clashed with Swanson (whose activities were transferred first to the East Coast studios, then to Paris, where she acquired a titled husband—a marquis—of her own). Negri was soon alienating Hollywood by declaring it a cultural wasteland beneath her contempt and ostentatiously retiring in solitude with her books and music to keep her company.

The public found her pretty silly. It was one thing to affect the queenly manner if it was well known that underneath you were just a Midwestern kid. Everyone knew Swanson was play-acting and everyone thought she had earned the right to her fantasies. Negri was just another foreign pretender—and stuck-up, at that.

When Negri hurtled cross-country to be at Valentino's deathbed it was the beginning of the end. They had indeed been lovers, and there is evidence that among his last words were, "Pola—if she does not come in time, tell her I think of her." But Negri laid on her grief a little too heavily, and shortly it became impossible to sell her films, despite expensive efforts to revamp the vamp's image. She married a prince of dubious standing, returned to Germany, which understood her, continued to make movies and, briefly, was linked with Hitler. "Why not?" she asked. "There have been many important men in my life—Valentino for example."

51

One of the poses typical of the star's eccentric orbit.

The rivals
MAE MURRAY

EVEN DIZZY LITTLE MAE MURRAY found herself a prince to marry—the brother of Negri's nobleman. By the time she did so, however, she had quite convinced herself that she was not of this world, so it would be both unkind and unjust to suggest that careerism or social climbing had anything to do with it. "I've always felt that my life touches another dimension," she sighed on one occasion, and an apparently reputable psychiatrist agreed with her. When the marriage to the prince—who turned out to be a bit of a beast—went bad, the good doctor told her, "You live in a world of your own," and he suggested that she might care to consult *Green Mansions* to find a literary parallel to her own case. Sure enough, in the enchanted Rima, Mae Murray saw herself.

She was a vague, fluttery, seemingly defenseless, oversensitive creature who, despite considerable evidence that she was born Marie Adrienne Koenig in Portsmouth, Virginia, insisted that she had always been Mae Murray and

The French Doll. *Miss Murray played the imaginative daughter of an antique dealer, acting out vignettes involving his wares.*

that she was born "on my father's boat whilst we were at sea." A great-grandmother, she said, had raised her, placing her in a series of European convents, in one of which she had been punished for dancing in the gardens at night. She was pretending that she was a firefly at the time, lighting matches as she whirled among the shrubbery.

The ethereal quality of her imagination remained a constant throughout her career. She insisted on mood music being played on the set while she was acting. She once bought some jewelry at Tiffany's and paid for it with little bags of gold dust. When Jack Gilbert stalked off the set of *The Merry Widow* after a dispute with director Erich Von Stroheim, she chased him out into the parking lot clad in nothing but her shoes. In short, the details of ordinary life were just too much for her to master. Probably the height of her impracticality was reached when, hearing that Paramount's East Coast office had recut one of her pictures, removing all its fairytale scenes, she boarded a train, *sans*

baggage, and headed for New York. There she spent weeks crawling about a warehouse, rescuing snippets of film from the cutting-room floor and pasting them back into the film.

That picture had been directed by her second husband, Robert Leonard, nicest of the three, but, according to Mae, insanely jealous of her. It was after their marriage broke up that she acquired her nobleman. With him she had a son —Koran, of all names—and with him she encountered career and money difficulties. Perhaps the public tired of her empty artiness, perhaps her well-publicized eccentricities swung opinion against her or maybe only Leonard really knew how to tailor a picture to her special talents. When the movies were finished with her, she retreated back to the Broadway musicals from which she had sprung. She now lives in retirement in Hollywood. Last year on a television program she said she thought Steve Reeves was the only current movie personality who matched those of her day. In a way, of course, she is right.

CLARA BOW
It can happen here

Vainly, she tried to teach her elders to dance on the edge of a volcano. The name of the picture is Mantrap.

CLARA BOW: "SHE DANCED even when her feet were not moving," said Adolph Zukor. "Some part of her was in motion in all her waking moments—if only her great rolling eyes." Madame Elinor Glyn, pronounced her the greatest living example of It, which cruder minds took to be merely sex appeal. She had that, of course, but something more was present—elemental magnetism, some said; animal vitality, others called it. No matter. She had the ability to express a restless youth's superficial aspect—the delight in movement without thought of goal, a craving for fun, jazzy, desperate, self-concealing fun.

She was a cute little flapper, bird-brained, glassy-eyed, a jangle to the nerves, a restlessness in the mind, a Charleston in the night-streets of a suburb. Among the heavy-breathing, comically serious "artists" of the silent screen she was like a sudden chorus of *Jada* at a Wagnerian opera.

She wanted to be a movie star more than anything else, and her father entered her photo in a fan magazine beauty contest. The prize was a part in a movie—and it was left on the cutting-room floor. There followed some quickie work, a trip across country to test for B. P. Schulberg, stardom as the girl Scott Fitzgerald always seemed to be writing about.

Sound, and nasty publicity about the results of her off-screen restlessness, ruined her. But as late as 1951, in good flapper fashion, she professed no regrets. From the twilight of a sanitarium room she declared: "We had individuality. We did as we pleased. We stayed up late. We dressed the way we wanted. I'd whiz down Sunset Boulevard in my open Kissel . . . with several red chow dogs to match my hair. Today, they're sensible and end up with better health. But we had more fun."

Clara Bow's fame was her only identity, and there were those who said she was a lonely girl, desperately fighting the feeling that she was unwanted. There are those who say that this was true of her entire generation.

Four people in Hollywood had "It," said Elinor Glyn:
actor Tony Moreno; Rex, the wild stallion;
the Ambassador Hotel doorman; and Clara Bow.

WALLACE REID

BEAUTIFUL WALLACE REID came to Hollywood with his father, Hal, a playwright, thinking he might like to become a cameraman. Someone, however, had the wit to strip him down to a breechcloth to play an Indian in *The Deerslayer*. Then Jesse Lasky spotted him playing a blacksmith in *The Birth of a Nation*, signed him and kept him under contract for the eight years it took him to rise and fall. He had, Lasky recalls, "a keen sense of humor, a good singing voice, he played the saxophone and piano and was altogether the most magnetic, charming, personable, handsome young man I've ever met. And the most cooperative."

In short, he was a nice guy, an average sort of man, with the average man's total lack of equipment for coping with sudden success. His screen personality was very like his real one, and he generally played good-natured, brotherly sorts. He made no strongly individual statement as a star. He was merely the best of the chisel-chinned, perfectly profiled, heavily brilliantined young leading men of the time. The combination of an ordinary manner with extraordinary looks was then, as now, a screen staple. It was both flattering and reassuring to the audience.

It was probably this very ordinariness that was Reid's undoing. Under pressure, he made too many pictures too quickly, and his life as a star was too difficult for him to fully comprehend and manage. His end began in 1920 in New York, where he was making *Forever*. Suffering from insomnia, exhaustion, anxiety and the bootleg booze he had been using as a prop for his ego, he began taking morphine so that he could face the camera (and the heat and glare of the klieg lights, which bothered many screen performers in those days) with some degree of poise. Before long, he was hooked.

The story of his addiction broke simultaneously with the trials of Fatty Arbuckle, the adroit Mack Sennett comedian charged with manslaughter, and the strange, rumor-ridden murder of William Desmond Taylor, a top director. Of the two cases, Arbuckle's was the more sordid. In the course of a midday drinking party in San Francisco, Arbuckle had escorted a minor actress named Virginia Rappe into another room and there had had sexual relations with her. Four days later she died of peritonitis caused by a ruptured bladder. The state charged that Arbuckle, in the course of his sexual adventure, had induced the fatal wound. It took three trials (there were two hung juries) to clear Arbuckle of the criminal charges, and in the course of them the courts heard, and the press lovingly reported, a succession of ex-

Wallace Reid as he appeared in Joan the Woman *opposite Geraldine Farrar and under the direction of DeMille in 1917.*

The hero as victim

remely unpleasant details about the nature of Fatty's party and its course on the fatal day. These confirmed everyone's worst suspicions about the quality of life in Hollywood.

Envious resentment had been growing, along with vicarious pleasure, as the star system grew. The resentments, based on the fame and money which were suddenly pressed upon the stars merely for existing—not for doing anything the puritan segment of the nation could justify as useful—needed only an Arbuckle case to focus upon. The press, of course, fed these as readily as it had fed the nation's need for gossip.

Just as Fatty, his career already ruined, went to trial for the last time, the Taylor story broke. His murder went unsolved, but in their investigations the police discovered that Mabel Normand—quite innocently—had visited Taylor the day before. Then they found that Mary Miles Minter, the virginal heroine of Chaplin films, had been inordinately fond of Taylor, who was twice her age. She might have lived this down had she not staged a particularly gauche scene at Taylor's funeral, embracing his body and claiming afterward that he had whispered to her, "I love you, Mary." People could not square this with her screen personality any more easily than they could Arbuckle's behavior with

his. She was ruined. Miss Normand, a truly delightful comedienne, survived professionally until, three years later, a man was killed in a brawl over her favors.

Hollywood desperately hired Will Hays, not so much to clean up film content (that came later) as to scrub its image. The very presence of square, starchy Hays on the scene helped, as did Cecil B. DeMille's production of *The Ten Commandments*, first of the Biblical epics. Finally, Wallace Reid performed his greatest service for the screen when he died, in 1923, in the sanitarium where he had gone for one last, desperate attempt to free himself from narcotics. "I'll either come out cured or I won't come out," he had said.

Mrs. Reid, who promptly made—with Hays's covert assistance—a film exposé of the narcotics habit, blamed the tragedy on the bad habits Reid had acquired from "his Bohemian friends" and got up a fund for a memorial chapel in New York's Cathedral of St. John the Divine. The industry made up a list of 117 players whose private lives were "unsafe," inserted morals clauses in all contracts and hoped the stars would behave themselves. What would happen next, author Elinor Glyn was asked. "Whatever will bring in the most money will happen," she replied sagely.

Reid in a highly symbolic still from The Charm School, *just prior to his fall from grace.*

NORMA and DOLORES

Norma Talmadge—"Thank God for the trust funds."

Norma Talmadge—"Thank God for the trust funds."

BUT EVEN AMIDST SCANDAL, the essential Hollywood flourished. And, nothing being more essential to it than girls, here are four of them—none truly a star of the first magnitude, yet all with a demonstrable ability to survive and, in varying degrees, to prosper. In their careers can be read some curious lessons about stardom and its nature.

Norma Talmadge was what can be described only as a pseudo actress. After her days as a Biograph leading lady—very much in the Pickford mold (as who was not in those days?)—she tended to specialize in parts requiring her to cry a great deal and to age considerably. The ability to do both is widely believed by movie audiences to be *per se* evidence of acting talent and, since frequently not even this much is required of the female screen star, they may be correct. At any rate Miss Talmadge and her sister Constance—who had a belle-of-the-ball quality and who generally played lighter parts than her more determined older sister—prospered during the twenties. Both had begun as teen-agers, products of the spirited urgings of a stage mother of the classic type. Norma married Joseph Schenck at this time and, like many less talented women, found marriage to an industry leader (he was president of United Artists) a considerable aid to the extension of her career at the head of the second rank. When sound entered, Constance quit the movies and wired her sister, "Leave them while you're looking good and thank God for the trust funds Momma set up." Norma, however, felt she must prove herself and, after a year of voice training, made her sound debut in 1930, with some success. Her second talkie, *Madame Dubarry*, fared poorly, and after its failure, she quit.

One of her costars in *Dubarry* was Dolores Del Rio, one of the most beautiful women in screen history. She was one of the very few actresses from south of the border to achieve any sort of career in Hollywood. Unlike her European counterparts, however, she was never cast as a vamp. Rather, she played "an assortment of puzzled Indian and Polynesian maidens." A wealthy and well-bred girl, she may have been the victim of southern California stereotyping, which finds a woman of Miss Del Rio's obvious qualities at variance with

Dolores Del Rio—perhaps her era's greatest beauty.

DOLORES and NORMA

Dolores Costello in a typically winsome pose.

its cultural attitudes toward Mexicans. Or it may have been that she was simply too beautiful and intelligent to be cast in the right sort of roles; it is only recently that beauties in the truly classic mold have achieved stardom—a touch of the common has long been widely regarded as essential for audience identification. In any case, Miss Del Rio had precious few good parts—a nice bit in *What Price Glory?*, even better roles in *Journey into Fear* and *The Fugitive* (both twenty years later). She was forced to return to her native land to achieve full-scale recognition. Recently she played a part on television and commented, "I took the part because it permitted me to play an intelligent, sensitive woman of character." The implication of her statement speaks volumes.

The other Dolores (Costello) should, perhaps, have done better than she did in Hollywood. She was the daughter of a distinguished theatrical family, and she was the wife of John Barrymore, who sensed in her a naturalness that was indeed the quality she best projected on the screen. "She walked into the studio like a charming child," Barrymore recalled. "Slender and shy and golden-haired. Never saw such radiance. My God! I knew that she was the one I had been waiting for. Waiting all my life, just for her." Barrymore promoted her career determinedly, but, in truth the times were against him. She was not right for romantic or flapper roles or as the hard and brittle women who became fashionable on the screen in the early thirties. She is representative of all the bright, brief careers that have flashed, then quickly flickered out in Hollywood.

Norma Shearer proved much more adaptable. She was hard-working, dependable, ambitious, bright, less beautiful than the average star, and not a strong personality. She got her start in short comedies, worked as a model, came to M-G-M for $150 a week, made eight films in her first year, mostly on loan-out, finally made her way all the way up the ladder when she married production chief Irving Thalberg. She too became an aspiring actress, even essaying Shake-

Late Shearer—in Robert Sherwood's Idiot's Delight.

speare's Juliet in one of the ventures into literature Thalberg so frequently undertook. He died in 1936, and without him her career did not fare well. She turned down two pictures— *Gone With the Wind* and *Mrs. Miniver*—that would have, to say the least, revived her career, and she made, instead, films that were either trifles or ponderous bores. Her last two films failed miserably, and she said later, "On those last two, no one but myself was trying to do me in."

What meanings are we to take from all this? The most ob-

vious is that the right connections can mean a great deal to a career, though not everything as Miss Costello proved. It is equally clear that mismanagement can prevent one from fully realizing potential (Miss Del Rio) and that it can quickly destroy an established career (Miss Shearer). Finally the Misses Shearer and Talmadge prove that the ability to resist type-casting, while it may prevent one from being a top star, can unquestionably preserve an unspectacular talent longer than one might believe possible.

Barrymore as he appeared on the stage.

BARRYMORE
The actor as star

In 1926, SHORTLY AFTER HE came to Hollywood, John Barrymore wrote to a friend in New York, "The most wonderful accident that ever happened to me was my coming out to this God-given, vital, youthful, sunny place." Barrymore was, at the time, forty-four—rather elderly to be casting his lot definitively with the movies. Already lapses of memory, perhaps the result of drinking, had begun to plague him, and there is no doubt that his taking up residence in Hollywood was mostly motivated by negative reasons—the desire to escape New York, scene of his recent divorce from Michael Strange, and the need, always chronic with him, for more money. His greatest triumph, his *Hamlet* of 1922-23 was only three years behind him, but it had drained him (he never again undertook a part of comparable difficulty), and he regarded the Hollywood trip as both an adventure and a restorative—which for a time it was.

He was a veteran of some fifteen films when he came to the Coast. None of them, with the exception of *Dr. Jekyll and Mr. Hyde,* had been particularly notable; and the silents

The star at ease in his Hollywood home.

Three stages of the Barrymore career.
Above, the perfect leading man
in The Beloved Rogue. *Right, the Great
Profile blurred, he continued to
work throughout the thirties as a
character actor, frequently parodying
his former screen self.*

64

he made after 1925—*The Sea Beast, Don Juan, When a Man Loves, The Magnificent Rogue*—added little to his luster. His style, however, was eminently suitable to the romantic dramas of the time, grand without being overbearing, intelligent but not lacking in a certain dash, vigor and humor. Heywood Broun noted that he entered a movie scene "like an exquisite paper knife"; and it was an apt description. There was an intelligence and control in his work as a leading man generally lacking in that of his contemporaries.

There is evidence, too, that he was temporarily happy. His love for young Dolores Costello had a revitalizing effect on him, as did the possession of a new yacht, *The Mariner*, which he seemed to regard as an expression of his true self in the midst of Hollywood's phoniness. His presence in pictures lent a cachet to the entire industry, and he was well worth the $76,250 he received for each of them.

Still, John Barrymore's career as a film actor would have been no more than a footnote in either his own record of achievement or Hollywood's history, had it not been for the fact that he acted out before the motion-picture audience the final scenes in the drama of his self-destruction. By 1930, as he approached fifty and as Hollywood went into its sound-inspired panic, the Great Profile began to soften and blur; his cheeks became slightly puffy, the clean line of his jaw began to sag, and a small but obvious dewlap developed beneath his chin. By the middle of the decade his marriage to Miss Costello was at an end, his earning capacity was severely impaired, and both his drinking and his lapses of memory had become chronic.

A Barrymore film now also offered a kind of horrified fascination—had the star slipped another notch, was he holding his own in his battle with this lingering illness of the spirit or was he, as sometimes happened (most notably in *Grand Hotel* and *Bill of Divorcement*), actually rallying? More and more, during the thirties, he played a parody of himself—an aging ham actor, a posturing drunk. Nowhere was this more bitterly revealed than in *Dinner at Eight*, an all-star production of 1933. His performance was not really good, but rarely has there been a more interesting one in the movies. Barrymore knew full well that he was playing his latter-day self, yet, throughout, he attempted to keep his distance from that self—in effect, to play another actor engaged to play John Barrymore. The attempt was brave and the younger Barrymore might have succeeded in this Pirandellian trick. Here it was quite beyond him, although he did create a kind of pathetic dignity as an actor who, in a single day, loses all self-illusions and, in a drunken attempt at a brilliant exit, commits suicide, carefully arranging the lighting of the scene before turning on the gas.

Within a few years, and despite the best efforts of friends to find him work, Barrymore, who by this time had to have his lines written out on slates and held before him out of camera range, could find no work but as this parody person. The most notable thing about his screen presence at the time was the distance in his eyes, which seemed never to be quite focused on anything. They seemed veiled, as if to protect the actor from knowledge of what he was doing, and to be looking far beyond the work at hand, perhaps back into the triumphant and profligate past, perhaps searching for a clue to this wretched present—or maybe they were merely trying to read the cue cards held up in the glare of the set. One thing is certain: never has our insistence on seizing hold of one aspect of a man's character and creating from it an immutable screen personality had more tragic results. Barrymore died May 29, 1942, of a complex of illnesses, a talented man forced into one of the most devastating self-exposures in the history of an art based on the display of the self.

The strange ways of immortality:
Barrymore signs his name in concrete
at Grauman's Chinese Theater.

JOAN CRAWFORD
The star as star

I Live My Life *was the appropriate title of the picture.*

JERRY WALD, THE INDEFATIGABLY EBULLIENT producer, was discussing the institution of stardom recently and remarked: "One gal I really respect is Joan Crawford. Crawford the Indomitable. Whether she's on the set or on the street or plugging a picture or plugging Pepsi-Cola, she's a star. That's her profession and she never lets you down."

Her only definition is as a star. You cannot extract from her work on the screen anything, a mannerism, a gesture, a habit of speech which betrays the "real" Joan. When she sweeps into the frame of a film we see not the entrance of a character, but the entrance of that curious abstraction— the movie star. When she "acts" she subtly communicates the fact that that is what she is doing. "Watch this," she seems to say, "I'm going to act for you now—and it's going to be great."

She came to Hollywood in 1925, an ex-chorine named Lucille Le Sueur who had had a nasty, poverty-stricken childhood under the name of Billie Cassin. Her screen name was created for her, in a fan magazine contest, by a Rochester housewife. Pudgy and rather bland, there seemed little reason to expect anyone to pick up her options for very long. But no sooner had she arrived at M-G-M than she began the process of creating herself. For months she nibbled on a diet consisting mainly of crackers, starving herself down to that eminently photographable angularity of face and figure which was to be the foundation of her longevity. In the process, her eyes—large, rolling, with just a hint of hysteria in them—first took on the importance they now have in her physiognomy.

Psychologically, her major asset has always been adaptability. There has never been time to get tired of Joan Crawford, because a new one is always being unveiled. Her first major success came in 1928, in *Our Dancing Daughters*, with its famous Charleston sequence. She followed this with a number of flaming-youth films, modulating into the confession films that were such a vogue in the early thirties. She overmatched herself in *Rain* (as Sadie Thompson), then seemed to idle along, not quite at top speed, alternating between musicals and undistinguished problem dramas through the rest of the decade. She was a star in name only. That is to say, her name was displayed above the title on any number of films, but none of them were important pictures. Formula films, they disappeared from memory almost as soon as the audience left the theater. Miss Crawford was just another second-stringer at Metro, which at the time had the best bench in the business. It was during this era that she was like a chameleon clinging to a slippery perch. Let someone else begin a film cycle and you could be certain that Joan Crawford would be in the second or third film in the

The youthful Crawford in a sequel to Our Dancing Daughters *called* Our Blushing Brides (left). *The more mature actress suffers schizophrenia in* Possessed *(1947).*

*The eyes have always had it. In 1932 they looked wildly
askance at Walter Huston's lustful preacher in* Rain.
*In 1954 they expressed the terror of a wealthy woman
who discovers that her youthful husband plans
to murder her. The name of the film is* Sudden Fear.

hung on.

Finally, in 1943, she left M-G-M for Warner's, and it was
at that point that she began at last to emerge as a remarkable
phenomenon. There was a hiatus while her new studio
fiddled around, looking for vehicles for her. The rumor that
they were looking for a graceful way to drop her began to
spread. "Let them try," she snarled. Two years later she
made *Mildred Pierce*, fittingly enough, the tale of an utterly
determined woman, fighting to improve herself economically
and socially, desperately putting aside humble origins, ba-
nality, ordinariness, to claw out for herself a position as a
top woman executive (and losing her chance for love in the
process). It might have been called *The Joan Crawford
Story*. For her performance she received the Academy
Award.

Then followed the series of pictures in which the star has
unforgettably limned the outlines of the American Woman
in the throes of status panic. In the process, at last, she
achieved the identity which had so long been denied her.
Her career is a tale of tenacity, and although she has yet to
appear on anyone's list of great actresses or even favorite
screen personalities, one can scarcely avoid going to her
films. One goes to be in the presence of a miracle. "How
does she do it?" you ask. And also, frequently, "What am
I doing here?"

Joan Crawford is an American phenomenon, the incredibly strong and determined woman, and at the box office we
pay tribute to her shrewd, single-minded, unwavering pursuit
of success. She lacks genuine appeal to men, but, because of
the special nature of her career she is the master of what

he trade knows as the "woman's picture." In these she suffers incredible agonies of the spirit in her attempts to achieve love and/or success, and her natural desire for these is constantly played upon by men of the nastiest sort—would-be gigolos, aging roués, frauds—all of whom offer her temporary surcease from loneliness, but at a terrible price to her dignity, and without proffering ultimate satisfaction. The women suffer along with Miss Crawford, but are reassured by what they know of her own career, which clearly states that a woman can triumph in a man's world.

As for Crawford herself, she carries herself with pride in herself and in her chosen profession—stardom. Once her pet poodle made himself very sick by nibbling on a carpet at Republic studios. "Cliquot was always happy when I was at the glamorous studios, like M-G-M and Warner Brothers," said Miss Crawford. "But when I went to Republic [definitely a second-rate operation] he got into trouble. Cliquot is miserable when I'm not working. When we go to a studio he is very happy." Cliquot obviously learned his moods somewhere.

Humphrey Bogart once growled, "The words 'movie stars' are so misused that they have no meaning. Any little pinhead who makes one picture is a star. Gable is a star. Cooper is a star, Joan Crawford, as much as I dislike the lady, is a star. . . . To be a star you have to drag your weight into the box office and be recognized wherever you go." Joan Crawford is a star because she says she is and because she has, through the years, insisted on the point so repeatedly and so firmly that the studios and the audience in general have finally conceded the point.

LON CHANEY
Genius without profile

LON CHANEY WAS KNOWN AS "the man of a thousand faces," but it would be more precise to say that he was a man with no face at all. In this sense, he was the most remarkable star the American screen has ever produced, offering his audience no recognizable traits of personality, even of face or body, with which they could identify. The child of deaf-mute ·parents he early achieved mastery of pantomine as a means of communication. A silent, publicity-shy man he relied only on this talent to establish human communion with his audience. Through it he created the aura of humanity that surrounded his most physically repulsive characterizations. Nearly always, the real Chaney hid behind grotesque (but masterfully created) make-up. Frequently he strapped his body into horribly contorted, tremendously painful positions to simulate the twisted, mutilated bodies of the people he portrayed. By rights he should have been merely another Hollywood character actor; that he achieved stardom is a tribute to his mimetic gifts. For however he racked his body, however much make-up he applied, he remained a recognizable human being. Never once were his afflictions attributed to supernatural causes. Never once did he fail to communicate the essential fact that, whatever had been done to him, he remained a man, a man capable of feeling, even of love. In his films, decent people turned away from him in fright and in horror; but in nearly all of them, someone— usually a character of great simplicity—accepted him on his own terms, saw beneath the monster to the man within. Chaney offered a challenge to his audience—would it turn away in disgust or open its heart? For the most part, it responded, classically, with pity and terror. In the aftermath of war, with disgust for man's inhumanity to man at its highest pitch in twentieth-century America, Chaney in his various deformed incarnations taught two prized lessons. The first was that there was no depth to the horror man could perpetrate on his fellows. The second was that an open, sympathetic heart could do much to salve these wounds and perhaps see that they would not happen again.

70

Chaney worked as a bit player in prewar films, achieved stardom in The Miracle Man
(1920), greatness in The Hunchback of Notre Dame (above).

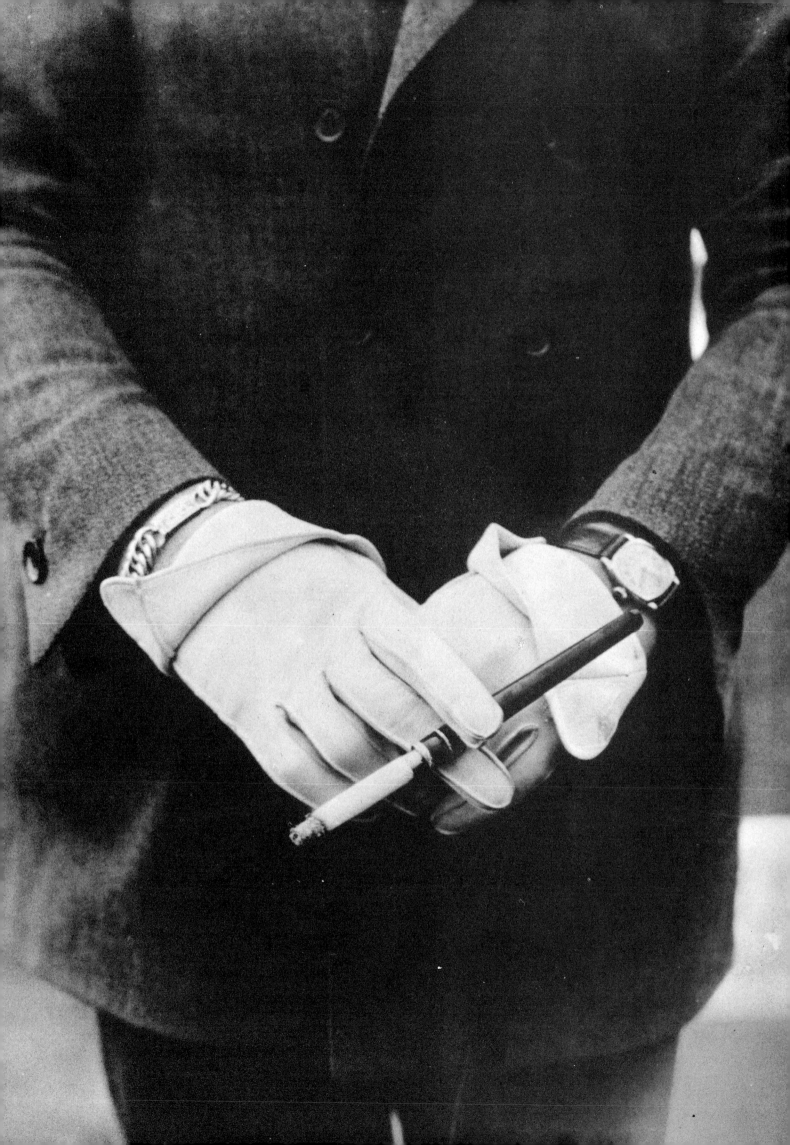

ERICH VON STROHEIM
Genius without portfolio

The star: Between takes with his son.

The Director: On location in Death Valley, shooting Greed.

IT WAS SAID THAT Erich Von Stroheim's mother had been a lady in waiting to the Empress of Austria, that his father had been a colonel of dragoons. This may or may not have been true, but one thing was certain: as an actor he was the perfect incarnation of the Teutonic military spirit, perfectly projecting that lustful blend of sadism and sentimentality which marks the type. Just how he got to Hollywood—and why he came—is not clear, but he was first noticed as an assistant to Griffith. He had his first vogue as an actor during World War I, when, almost single-handedly, he created the home front's image of what it was fighting against.

When the war ended, and with it the market for his services, Von Stroheim convinced Carl Laemmle of Universal that he ought to be a director, and for him he made the first of his several masterpieces, *Blind Husbands*. It was a smash hit, rescued Universal from a desperate financial situation and, most important, brought degeneracy to the screen. This film, like his others, had an unblinking realism, a rightness of detail that bespoke, if not intimate knowledge, then an instinctive feeling for the mood of an aristocracy in decline.

Von Stroheim was the poet of lust in all its forms and all of his films were striking visual metaphors about the effect on men of this most degrading of the deadly sins. Alas, Von

Stroheim behind the camera was as brutal and as profligate as one of his own characters. The stories of his excesses have become Hollywood legend—how he kept an entire company waiting twenty hours for a dog to sneeze (four extras fainted); how he ordered the underwear of extras (which would never be seen on screen) embroidered with a coat of arms; how he shot fifty reels of film for a picture that could not use more than ten of them.

His downfall was *Greed*. Until then he had laid his scenes in Europe, well-known by Americans to be in the final agony of payment for its sins. Now he turned to America and demonstrated that it was as debauched as the Austro-Hungarian Empire. Released in a butchered, but still brilliant version, it was offensive to the comparatively few Americans who saw it; in an uneasily materialistic decade, the picture tapped a guilty national conscience. Von Stroheim directed a few more films, worked occasionally as an actor, made a brief comeback portraying the hated Hun in World War II movies and another in *Sunset Boulevard* (1950). A movie genius, and a genius at self-destruction, he died in Paris in 1957, exiled from the American industry, which had never understood him and which therefore feared him too much to make intelligent use of his talent.

The essence of "the man you love to hate."

73

TOM MIX
Cowboy to an age

Mix comes perilously close to riding sidesaddle.

THERE MUST BE A COWBOY, and cowboy to the era of wonderful nonsense was Tom Mix. His presence was enough to make the disciple of pure Western form shudder. He habitually appeared in public dressed all in white, and his home rivaled Valentino's *Falcon's Lair* and Doug and Mary's *Pickfair* in ostentation. Its embellishments could have occurred only to a cowboy who, after a long, hard winter hits town and sweeps the table in a poker game grander than the imagination can bear. Atop his house, lights flung a challenge to the heavens, spelling out his name in letters taller than a man. Inside there was a fountain that sprayed water alternately blue, pink, green, red. When Samuel Goldwyn gave Vilma Banky and Rod LaRocque the wedding to end all weddings, Mix drove to it in a coach-and-four—probably something of an inconvenience for a man whose auto contained a complete bar. He publicly showered his wife and his daughter, Thomasina, with jeweled gifts to rival

those of a potentate, and he still had enough money to retire completely when sound came.

With all of this, he was, technically speaking, the most proficient horseman in movie history. Born in Mix Run, Pennsylvania, he had gone west at an early age, was twice a real-life sheriff and was a Texas Ranger for three years. In addition, he had been a soldier of fortune in the Boer War and had served in the United States Army both in the Spanish-American War and in the Boxer Rebellion. He made his first movie in Oklahoma in 1910, when the Selig Company, out of Chicago on location, hired him as an extra. He was a minor Western star before and during the time William S. Hart was casting the screen stereotype of the Man of the West. It was not until Hart fell out of step with his time that Mix became the ranking screen cowboy.

His version of the West was much more romanticized than Hart's. Realism bored him, and the idea of being anything as subtle as a good bad man was quite beyond him. The West was, for him, merely an abstraction, a convenient, stylized backdrop against which to act out his simple dramas of heroism. He was, on the screen, a puritan of the plains, tempted neither by bad women nor good whiskey.

Nevertheless, the real Westerners who acted as extras and stunt men in Hollywood productions preferred riding with him to riding with Hart, who was less adept than Mix when atop a horse. An able stunt man, Mix never used doubles and was perfectly capable of galloping his horse, Tony, through a cattle stampede, throwing the animal next to his imperiled heroine, always a rather bland little creature, at precisely the right moment, then sheltering her in the lee of the horse while the herd thundered by.

He had that kind of empty bravery—the bravery of the soldier of fortune, the man for whom risk is an end in itself. He lacked Hart's feeling for—and of—the Old West. Like most of his audience, Mix felt no regret at its passing. He felt no need for a sense of place, no need for roots. The thrill of the moment was enough for him—that and his name in lights ten feet tall, reassuring him as to his fame but not, alas, guaranteeing him a distinguished immortality.

The house that Tom built, fit for a cattle baron, but not for a cowboy.

Charles Farrell and Janet Gaynor in Street Angel.

MALE AND FEMALE

THE HISTORY OF LOVE TEAMS is almost as long as that of the movies in America. The first of any importance was that of wooden Francis X. Bushman and Beverly Bayne, who, prior to World War I, kept their real-life marriage secret lest it destroy the illusions of their fans. They needn't have bothered, for the secret of the love team's success lies in the inevitability of its members coming together in the last reel.

Inevitability is a subject not often discussed by motion-picture critics, who set great store by novelty. But the truth is that both the star system and the construction of the average film depend on giving people, if not what they want, then what they have been led, by experience, to expect. The excellent American film is one which works highly original variations within the stylization demanded by the half dozen or so time-tested genres that account for most of our production. How else can one explain the very real sense of disappointment one feels when, somehow, the wrong—that is to say, the novel—ending suddenly appears in the last reel? Only Alfred Hitchcock, who has assiduously cultivated the idea that his films will always have a surprise ending, and who therefore leads us into the theater *expecting* a trick, can get away with it.

The presence of Colman and Banky, Farrell and Gaynor in a movie was an absolute guarantee that the movie would meet all preconceived notions of how a romance should end. The coming of sound cut off the Colman-Banky liaison just as it was about to become an institution. Hungarian-born Vilma Banky simply could not master the intricacies of English, and since she was happily married to Rod LaRocque, she went off to Europe and made a few films with him, after which the two settled down to a comfortable, easy-going

Ronald Colman and Vilma Banky in One Night of Love.

semi-retirement in Hollywood. Her only genuine difference from the other vamps was that she was blonde and they tended to be dark.

Colman, of course, with his well-tuned British accent, prospered mightily in sound pictures. He was, in the words of one observer, "the middle-aged woman's hope and despair." The romances of the love teams were indeed aimed at an older audience, an audience not seeking identification so much as it was the restoration of belief.

Colman and Banky cavorted in Graustarkian situations, by and large, but Charles Farrell and Janet Gaynor, who co-starred for over seven years, were quite a different thing. They were "average"—in the sense that the characters in soap operas are said to be average. Farrell was, in the words of a competitor, "the oldest choirboy," just as Miss Gaynor was, until her memorable appearance in *A Star Is Born* (1937), the oldest schoolgirl. Undoubtedly they offered a false nostalgia, recalling the fun, romance and heartaches of young love, which moviegoers delightedly imagined had been part of their own early lives.

It is perhaps a measure of the slightly-increased sophistication of screen content that there are no love teams now working with the steadiness that these did, and that no pairing of actress and actor has achieved the kind of adulation that these and the greatest team of them all, Gilbert and Garbo, achieved.

Gilbert, Garbo, grapes in Queen Christina, *one of his comeback attempts.*

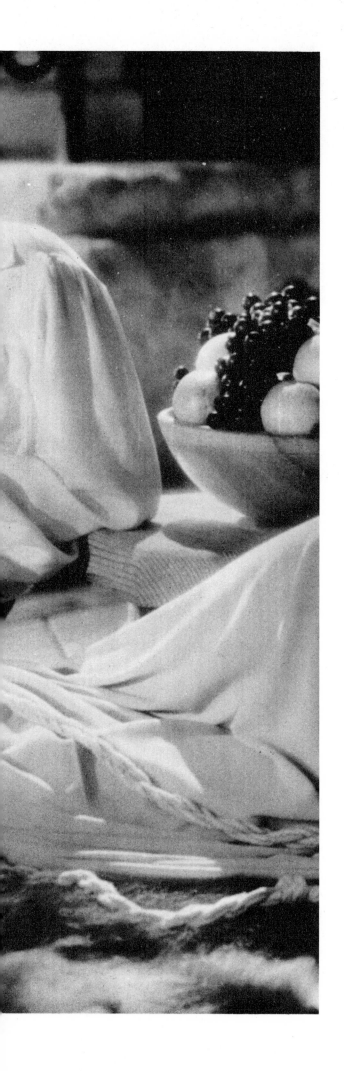

GILBERT and GARBO

ADELA ROGERS ST. JOHN WROTE that "in the full flower of their romance, Gilbert and Garbo were added by movie fans to the list of immortal lovers, Romeo and Juliet, Dante and Beatrice, Anthony and Cleopatra. They portrayed love between man and woman as Shakespeare wrote it in his sonnets to the Dark Lady." They were, indeed, a perfect combination on screen—Garbo, the enigma; Gilbert, the clever and sophisticated boudoir strategist, the one man in the world capable of penetrating the enigma. The scenes between them have the fascination of a duel, erotic tension building between them until the lady's ultimate capitulation, and extending through the afterglow, which lasts for several scenes. Against the stylized absurdities of their backgrounds, and despite the nonsensical plots which brought the two together, Gilbert and Garbo created real romance, an intimacy which belied the fantasy surrounding them.

In this work they were undoubtedly aided by the general knowledge that they were off-screen lovers. Gilbert, who, according to a friend, "had a tendency to overcapitalize romance both on the screen and off," brought enthusiasm and therefore believability to his work in the love scenes. Essentially a troubled, not terribly bright man, he apparently carried a torch for Garbo for many years. She, according to reliable reports, loved him for exactly fourteen days, although twice she seemed on the point of marrying him and was at some pain to extend the relationship on a just-good-friends basis for quite a while. In 1933, four years after their last silent film together, in the period of Gilbert's decline, she was instrumental in casting him in *Queen Christina*, partly for sentimental reasons, partly because he was eminently right for the part of her Spanish lover. Gilbert came to their love scenes with his customary ardor. Garbo suggested he tone them down. "Backward, turn backward, O Time, in your flight," Gilbert sighed in vain.

Gilbert as a family man in The White Circle.

John Gilbert was a contradictory personality. To some—especially those in the audience—he was a dashing, yet wholesome cavalier, a perfect figure of romance. To his friends he was gay, reckless, convivial, slightly mad in the manner of many stars. To his enemies, as numerous as his friends, he was conceited, rebellious, a spoiled child. One of them, former boxer Jim Tully wrote, "his emotion is on the surface. His nature is not deep. His enthusiasms are as transient as newspaper headlines."

Actually, Gilbert's behavior reflected a troubled, perhaps even bitter, man. The child of third-rate stock-company actors, he did not much like his profession. He had come to Hollywood hoping to direct and was frequently promised such work in order to lure him into acting parts that were distasteful to him. He was a minor star until, under Von Stroheim's direction, he triumphed in *The Merry Widow*. He followed this with an even more impressive performance in *The Big Parade*. "That was worth doing," he said. "All the rest was balderdash."

From this point on he was the biggest male star since Valentino. In him the two major male film personality styles of the time met. He could essay either the hearty good humor of the collar-ad types or the grace of the Latin lovers. Hence the ease with which he slipped from the American soldier's role in *Parade* to *Flesh and the Devil* with Garbo.

His tragedy, of course, was his voice. It is well-known that he signed a million-dollar contract with M-G-M just before the coming of sound, how badly his voice miked in the early, crude days of sound, making ludicrous the high-flown dialogue of his first talkie, *His Glorious Night*. Studio and friends tried to help him, no one attempted to cancel his contract, various vehicles were tried for him, but his voice continued to evoke snickers from the audience.

Always a heavy drinker, his consumption increased, and in 1935 he died of a heart attack. Oddly, when he died he may have been standing on the brink of a comeback. He had accepted a character role in a minor film and, as a drunken screen-writer, speaking naturalistic, rather cynical dialogue, his thin voice was actually an asset. It had apparently never occurred to anyone in sound-panicked Hollywood that while it is hard to change voices it is possible to change images and that playing a character more like himself, less like a fantasy construct, he might have survived sound.

GILBERT

His Glorious Night *with Catherine Dale Owen*
was John Gilbert's first talkie—and his downfall.
The famous "white voice" sounded surpassingly silly,
mouthing the high-flown romanticisms of the script.

GARBO

THE FACTS OF GRETA GUSTAFSSON'S early life ·are simple
enough. She was born in Stockholm, September 18, 1905,
the child of country people who had a hard time adjusting
to the life of the city. Her father, a quiet, handsome man,
was never able to provide his family with more than the bare
necessities of life. After he died in 1920, Greta went to work
as an apprentice in a barbershop (a fairly common choice of
work for Swedish girls), quickly left for an apprenticeship
in the millinery department of a large store. It was in this
job that she gained her first theatrical experience, appearing
in a short advertising film that the store prepared. After that
she did another, about the bakery business, for the same
director.

She had long held, and frequently talked about, an ambition to be an actress. So, in 1922, when the opportunity
came, she left the department store in order to appear in her
first professional film, a little knockabout comedy in the
Sennett manner. When it was finished she gained admit-
tance—with only the sketchiest of instruction to prepare her
for her audition—to the Royal Academy, training ground
for Swedish actors for two centuries. At the end of her first
term, the academy, responding to a call from Mauritz Stiller,
Sweden's leading film director and, with Victor Seastrom,
the creator of that nation's excellent reputation for trend-
setting art films, selected Greta and another student to audition for parts in *Gosta Berling's Saga.*

It is at this point that complexity enters the life of Greta
Gustafsson. Against everyone's advice, Stiller gave her the
second lead in that film. She was at the time shy, gawky,
both chubby and cherubic in appearance, but, possessing a
certain freshness of appeal which, while hardly notable, was
suitable for her part. Much more important, however, was a
passivity, a willingness to be molded, which fitted an obsession of Stiller's. He was in the grip of a dream—to find a
Galatea to whom he could play Pygmalion.

Like so many film directors of the era, Stiller had an
imperious ego, a desire to play (and a certain talent for)
the part of the cinematic master builder, the universal filmic
genius. Before finding young Greta Gustafsson, he had told

Garbo as Mata Hari.

friends of the ideal woman he was seeking—"supersensual, spiritual, mystic." If ever he could find such a person he would mold her into the greatest star of all time—a woman who could personify all women, or at least the romanticized and idealized woman whom artists had been celebrating for centuries. She would be, as he described her to a friend, "sophisticated, scornful, superior, but under the shining surface humanely warm and womanly." He also thought that she should be able to create, at least subliminally, an aura of enigmatic soulfulness. Long before he found the girl of his dream he had, with the aid of an assistant, concocted a name by which the world would know her. The name he chose was Garbo.

On the *Gosta Berling* set everyone wondered why Stiller was troubling so much with his new actress. Only a few realized that he had at last found the woman of his fantasies. A woman who worked at Svensk Filmindustri at the time recalled the making of a star for John Bainbridge, Garbo's best biographer. "She was really very attractive, especially her figure. That is what attracted people in Sweden, not her face. I can still see Stiller and that young girl—forever walking up and down, up and down, in the shade of that little grove just outside the studio. Stiller was always teaching and preaching, Greta solemnly listening and learning. I never saw anyone more earnest and eager to learn. With that hypnotic power he seemed to have over her, he could make her do extraordinary things. But we had little idea then that he was making over her very soul."

Perhaps the last sentence is hyperbolic, but the essence of the reminiscence is true. What followed is well enough recorded. After *Saga* was finished, she appeared under Stiller's direction in the German-financed *Street of Sorrows;* and Hollywood, in thrall to the new movie style being created on the Continent, hired Stiller as it had earlier obtained the services of Seastrom. Stiller made a contract for Garbo a condition of his signing. Louis B. Mayer, negotiating the deal, solemnly told Miss Garbo, through an interpreter, that she really ought to lose weight. "Tell her that in America men don't like fat women," he said. Garbo is reported to have smiled enigmatically at this advice.

With Stiller, she arrived in America in 1925, and there was no special excitement about the occasion. In fact, M-G-M had no idea, now that they had the Swedes, what to do with them. Stiller never completed a picture for the studio, although he did a couple for rival companies with no success and eventually retreated to Sweden. Garbo's screen test did not impress Irving Thalberg, who had just come to Metro from Universal, and it required a set of still photos plus a new screen test to illuminate for him and his fellow moguls the elusive, magical and (to this day) undefinable quality she had.

At any rate, they put her into *Torrent,* shocking and disappointing both Garbo and her mentor by not letting Stiller direct the film. The film, in retrospect, is quite poor (as indeed were all but a handful that Garbo made), but critics and public alike responded to the presence of the lady. Her second film, *The Temptress,* started under the direction of Stiller, but Fred Niblo, a handy hack, soon took over. This was the beginning of the end of Garbo's reliance on Stiller. In a very short time he would be back in Sweden, and the real building of the Garbo legend, based on her noted reticence, would begin.

This legend, let it be stated clearly, fit neatly with the somewhat mysterious screen presence of the star. The two fed each other. Nearly always, she was cast as a woman of mystery, somewhat somnambulistic, yet hinting at a promise of sexual adventure on a plane higher than ordinary people could even fantasy. Similarly, off screen, despite her mannish clothes and her carelessness of appearance, she was enigmatic. No one knew exactly how she spent her time, although there were always hints of the most interesting sorts of suitors. No one knew any details of her life, except that she lived frugally (using only a couple of rooms in her large home, borrowing the butler's newspaper to save a nickel, owning so few clothes that she could travel all the way to Europe with just one suitcase) and in a manner totally different from any other star. It may be that her ability to be different is one of the factors that account for the undying interest of intellectuals in her work. But, of course, there is more to the growth of the Garbo cult than that.

Alistair Cooke, the movement's unofficial recording secretary, called her "every man's harmless fantasy mistress. By being worshiped by the entire world she gave you the feeling that if your imagination has to sin, it can at least congratulate itself on its impeccable taste." Others called her "the supreme symbol of inscrutable tragedy." Still others "a super-human symbol of The Other Woman." Kenneth Tynan, writing long after Garbo's active career had ended, put it this way:

"What, when drunk, one sees in other women, one sees in Garbo sober. She is woman apprehended with all the pulsating clarity of one of Aldous Huxley's mescalin jags. To watch her is to achieve direct, cleansed perception of something which, like a flower or a fold of silk, is raptly, unassertively, and beautifully itself. . . . Tranced by the ecstasy of existing, she gives to each onlooker what he needs: her largesse is intarissable. . . . Fame, by insulating her against a multitude of experiences which we take for granted, has increased rather than diminished her capacity for wonder."

The transformation of Ninotchka: Before Melvyn Douglas shows her the delights of Western materialism . . .

. . . and after. Garbo laughs, completing the parody of what she had been.

Of all the attempts to explain the curious hold which Garbo has over the imagination of men, Tynan's is the best. He accepts her for exactly what she is—the ultimate movie star, a beautiful object to be admired and to be invested, like any work of art, with whatever private meanings we care to give her. The nature of our relationship to the stars having changed over the years since the screen began to talk, our admiration for her is, in a sense, atavistic. It is based on the fact that after speaking from the screen, she imposed upon herself, after the last movie (*Two-Faced Woman*, 1941), silence—a silence she has never broken. She was a goddess who became technologically unemployed and, rather than face life and a career as a merely mortal star of the new sort, she chose to preserve her mythic quality, which, of course, in our notably noisy society, means a form of isolation.

This is not to imply that Garbo's decision was an unnatural one, a perverse yet effective way of maintaining her place in the public eye. It is widely believed that Garbo is a trifle strange in her desire for privacy, but it is strange only in the context of the public life to which her fellow stars have acquiesced. "I never said 'I want to be alone,' " she said one time, "I only said 'I want to be *let* alone.' There is all the difference." How many stars have insisted on this point in interviews. How few of them could stand it if, suddenly, they were indeed let alone. It is in fundamental contradiction to the needs of the average performer's ego. But Miss Garbo's personality as a performer having been constructed for her mainly by Stiller, there is a certain logic in her falling back upon a cultural value—privacy—highly prized in her native land, especially in her class.

Miss Garbo is, apparently, as sturdy an individual, as ruggedly self-sufficient, as any of the five generations of rural, small-landholding Gustafssons who preceded her. She continues to have friends, is apparently at ease socially if no one refers to her life as an actress. She is fond of small antique shops, of an occasional afternoon at the movies, of unannounced visits to friends. She is, finally, one of the last devotees of that totally engaging activity, walking the streets of the city, observing its endlessly fascinating life. "Sometimes, I put on my coat at ten in the morning and go out and follow people," she said once. "I just go where they're going. I mill around." Oddly, and perhaps a little too crudely, one could say that like any successful person Garbo has achieved, by dint of hard work, even perseverance, a style of life which suits her.

What is left for a new generation is an attempt to understand precisely what she represented on the screen. Here Parker Tyler, in his brilliant, forgotten book, *The Hollywood Hallucination*, is a help. "Frigidity in a woman of beauty or charm is a direct challenge to male sexual vanity. Garbo's peculiar art has always been to say in essence to the male audience: 'Don't forget that I am only an image, and that is all I can be to you.' " So, beside Tynan's idea of the beautiful somnambule so enigmatic that she can be all things to all men (and women and children, as the script of one of her films has her say), one must set another, simpler image. At certain moments "her orthodox defenses are down, her will against seduction seems to melt, at last all her conscious, instinctive reluctance disappears. . . . A few moments of pantomime rehearse the basic natural drama of sexually uneducated women and sexually educating man."

In the eleven years during which she spoke, her power at the box office slowly diminished. The more she spoke the less enigmatic she became. Because of her hold on the imagination, her decline was slower than that of the other silent stars, but in the end her studio tried two desperate—and stupid—expedients. First they put her in *Ninotchka*, in which she, in effect, played her real self for the first time— distant, reserved, yet capable of warmth when correctly approached. In this film Melvyn Douglas, playing a perfect American type, finally accomplished what all others had failed to do—the sexual initiation of The Woman into American-type love making. Garbo had been taken before, but never cheerfully or without devastating consequences. Her fantasy value was destroyed. In the disastrous *Two-*

Faced Woman which followed, Garbo, now fully Americanized, was made to indulge in the kind of "cute" sex farce all too familiar to the moviegoer.

A Metro executive once remarked, wonderingly, "Garbo was the only one we could kill off, . . . the women seemed to enjoy watching Garbo die." But, of course. It was the very essence of her screen nature that, through death or distance, she remained beyond ordinary sexuality. Her films, until the end, were the retelling of incidents, brief encounters, in which the male temporarily penetrated her masklike beauty, made her react like a real woman, for which crime common form demanded punishment. To wantonly disturb this pattern was an aesthetic crime. There is reason to believe that Garbo knows her career was mismanaged, and that from time to time the knowledge still disturbs her.

The star as recluse: "Her life is . . . a file of newspaper pictures catching her aghast . . . on the gangplanks of ships or the stairways to planes."

THE

PART THREE

COMEDIANS

Buster Keaton in a moment of classic American folk art.

WHILE THE REST OF THE MOTION-PICTURE industry was turning out "art" that, in the final analysis, was utter nonsense, the comedians of the silent screen were creating nonsense that has now come to be recognized as genuine art. An entire, intelligent school of thought about popular culture has built a critical theory out of the truism that mass culture succeeds best precisely when it tries least. The best example they can cite is the work of the silent comics.

The comedians had few illusions about the nature of their work. They simply sought laughter and they did so in an interesting variety of ways, expressing a great deal of themselves in the course of this pursuit. The common element in

the style of the silent comics was, to use the word another way, commonness. They were rude, vulgar, rowdy, and extremely fast-moving operatives, for, if they had slowed down, giving the audience a chance to think, the joke might well have collapsed.

There are parallels to their work in the history of literary comedy in America, the main stream of which tends to be picaresque, grotesque and physical rather than intellectual in its humor. There are also parallels in the history of theatrical comedy. But it is perhaps enough to say of the humor practiced by the silent comedians that it was the product of a fortuitous coincidence of talent, time and medium, and that its practitioners are sorely missed today.

CHAPLIN

Tillie's Punctured Romance, *Marie Dressler playing the title role.*

"OH WELL, HE WAS just the greatest, that's all," said Mack Sennett of Charles Spencer Chaplin, and there is no disputing the fact. Chaplin came to the movies as a very young man, after a dismal life in England, where he had toured with his parents, who were low-class music hall performers, and had spent a good deal of time in an orphanage. His first success—and it was modest enough—came when he joined the Karno Comedy Company at seventeen. He played secondary parts but one of his routines, involving a tangle with a dog, was a success both in English and Continental music halls. He came to America with Karno's touring company and played three years with it before Sennet discovered him. At that time he was casting about for someone as a stand-by for his biggest star, Mack Swain, who was beginning to make heavy salary demands. Chaplin hesitated to leave the security of his job with Karno, where he was earning fifty dollars a week, and it was not until Sennett tripled that amount that he signed. At first he was lost among the rowdy Keystone clowns. His work is based, of course, on a delicate, almost balletic kind of pantomime, and on the Keystone lot it was widely believed that Chaplin was one of Sennett's mistakes.

It was Sennett's thrifty habit to borrow action for his films wherever he could, and so, one day he sent a crew and cast out to nearby Venice to improvise a comedy around some children's auto races. There Chaplin came into his own. He remembered a bit he had done when, working as a janitor in a London music hall, he had been pressed into service as a replacement for an ailing comedian. He had donned the huge comic's clothing and had tripped and stumbled through a routine that became a feature on the bill.

Now, on the day that *The Kid Auto Races at Venice* was filmed, he borrowed a pair of pants from Fatty Arbuckle, some equally outlandish shoes from Ford Sterling, a fake mustache from Swain, fell into the shuffling gait of an aged peddler he had seen in England and the outward aspect of his "Little Fellow" was presented on the screen for the first time. As for the inner fire of his creation—that incurable optimism in the face of disaster—that was pure Chaplin. "You have to believe in yourself, that's the secret," he once told one of his sons. "Even when I was in the orphanage, when I was roaming the streets trying to find enough to eat to keep alive, even then I thought of myself as the greatest actor in the world. I had to feel that exuberance that comes from utter confidence in yourself. Without it you go down to defeat."

Within three months of filming *The Kid Auto Races* he was directing his own films for Sennett, the only way he felt he could protect the Little Fellow. Even so, he chafed at the demands placed on him by Sennett's implacable production schedule. When another studio offered him more time to work on his films, as well as more money, he moved on. In 1916 he was offered a $670,000-a-year contract and made a tumultuous journey to New York to sign it. Wherever the train stopped, Chaplin was mobbed; in New York he was greeted like a conquering hero. He was Everyman, raised to the *n*th power. "I was loved by crowds," he later recalled, "but I didn't have a single close friend . . . I felt like the loneliest man alive." A year later he signed a contract which called for a million dollars a year in salary.

Chaplin in Carmen.

All
the
ills
of
man ...

With Jackie Coogan in The Kid.

...childre

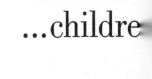
women...

With Paulette Goddard, then his wife, in The Great Dictator.

94

machinery...

Modern Times

The Great Dictator

tyranny...

age...

and...

The old vaudevillian of Limelight.

...war

*Chaplin in two wars: Above, at the
height of his power in* Shoulder Arms,
the lighthearted satire of World War I.

LONELINESS AND WEALTH remained constants in the troubled private life of Charles Chaplin. Yet his screen self, the Little Fellow, remained unchanged through the twenties; and, when sound came in, Chaplin managed to cling successfully to silence, producing two films, *City Lights* and *Modern Times*, which had sound tracks but no spoken dialogue. After that, however, it became impossible to retain the characterization with which by this time he, the actor, was inextricably entwined, both through art and the public's wish. For fifteen years the pictures had been appearing less and less frequently. Now, in the thirties, they ceased altogether as Chaplin turned to preparation for *The Great Dictator*. The picture, of course, contained scenes involving the Little Fellow, but it was not primarily his picture, and he has not reappeared in the three films Chaplin has since made.

It was society, not Chaplin, who killed off the beloved character. Robert Warshow shrewdly suggests that until the cataclysmic thirties the relationship between the tramp and the rest of the world was an innocent one. That is, they did not totally understand each other and they came into accidental conflict that was hilarious, but which had no serious moral tow. There was no viciousness in these conflicts, and if there was any message in the comedy it was simply, "live and let live."

But as fascism rose in Europe and as depression spread in America, it began to seem that there could no longer be any innocent conflict between the individual and his society. In both *Modern Times* and *The Great Dictator* the society through which the Little Fellow moves is actively malevolent; it is no longer attempting to persuade him into conformity, it is bent on destroying him. No longer can he shrug, adjust his pitiful raiment about him and set off down the road. The open dusty road itself is suddenly a superhighway and there is no place on it for The Tramp and his love of freedom. Chaplin seemed to lose faith in him as a symbol just as, coincidentally, the actor operating as an individualist on a slightly different plane entered upon the sea of troubles—legal, political and tax—that led to his embittered exile in Switzerland where he still lives.

Last of the Little Fellow: Chaplin donned the familiar costume for a few scenes in The Great Dictator, *but the world had grown too malevolent for The Tramp to survive.*

BUSTER KEATON

As Chaplin came to think of himself as an artist his films tended to take on a slower pace, their subsidiary characters a greater subtlety. Worse, as he began to lose faith in the applicability of the truth for which the Little Fellow stood, his films replaced their hard gleam of honesty with the softer glow of sentimentality. In Buster Keaton's work there was no slowness, subtlety or sentiment. Instead there was fantastic emphasis on high-speed timing; the inventiveness of his gags, which had the maniac precision of some infernal machine, are unsurpassed in film history. As for his character, it had no depth at all. It had no background, no discernible major goals and, therefore, no emotion.

Keaton, of course, is famous for his utterly dead pan. His face was a mask, hiding all emotion. The miracle was that no matter how his seemingly delicate person was assaulted he never cracked. He always pressed sternly forward, intent on just one thing—victory over the forces which, inexplicably had been loosed upon him. He was, in short, a comedian with precisely one joke in his repertory, that being his uncanny ability to take it without registering so much as surprise, let alone discouragement or disappointment with his peculiar lot. Within this arbitrary limit, however, he was marvelously inventive. One disaster led to another which in turn led to yet another still more horrid, all in a matter of seconds. We wait suspensefully for him to weep or to smile or to beg for mercy, yet he never does. He merely plods on until, at last, threatened man and machines suddenly give up their vain assault upon him, and he emerges victorious, disdaining even the victor's smile of triumph.

Keaton wins out for but one reason—his absolute unshakability. The uses of the deadpan at last become clear. It is the reverse of the petty salesman's mask against disaster —the fixed smile and false heartiness. As long as Keaton retained his expressionless aplomb he could not be reached. Had he once revealed emotion he would have presented his enemies with a chink through which they would have destroyed him. The result was a certain coldness in his screen character. But perhaps coldness—combined with determination—is the best means of survival in this world.

Buster Keaton finds himself in a typical contretemps in The Three Ages of Man, *the inevitable result of sailing alone.*

Plodding, implacable, he follows the antique adage,
Go West, Young Man.

99

Episodes in the short, unhappy screen life of Harry Langdon, who had an uncanny, fluttery ability to parody a child's panic at encountering the unknown.

The curious incident of the bicycle, in Long Pan

THE FACE HARRY LANGDON PRESENTED to disaster was total ly different from Keaton's. It was, as Agee suggests, the of an infant—and a rather unhealthy one at that—per manently arrested in the premoral stage. There was no calm ness here only ill-concealed panic. He was the master the panicky flutter when confronted, as he constantly was by danger. The point about Langdon, who sometimes ro to heights of almost surrealist madness his contemporari never attempted, was that, in direct opposition to Keato he was totally incompetent physically as well as menta and morally. Not knowing right from wrong he would t

The Chaser. *The hat, the uniform, the strange situation of the young lady are all equally inexplicable, especially to Langdon, who could never figure anything out.*

HARRY LANGDON

anything to extricate himself from his difficulties. Having not even the intelligence of an adolescent, he invariably chose the wrong course of action. He was the *reductio ad absurdum* of humanity. Indeed, in his tiny hat with its up-turned brim and in his oddly cut clothing, he seemed not to be human at all, but rather a fugitive from some back-ward planet placed on this earth and told to survive in the best possible way.

Langdon's director and chief screen mentor, Frank Capra, summed up the guiding principle a Langdon's comedy by saying, "His only ally was God. Langdon might be saved by the brick falling on the cop, but it was *verboten* that he in any way motivate the brick's fall." His competitors always extricated themselves from their troubles through their own devices, he never did.

Characteristically, Langdon messed up his own career. He quickly grew pretentious, began listening to various high-brow theorists who attached themselves to this strange, simple ex-vaudevillian, and his major work was finished in a few short years. He retreated to the two-reelers whence he had sprung, and he died broke in 1944.

101

Why Worry? *The Giant is real; so is Harold Lloyd's problem.*

HAROLD LLOYD

HAROLD LLOYD WAS THE MOST POPULAR comedian of his time, and it is said that, all told, his films grossed over thirty million dollars. He was the least enigmatic of the great clowns, always portraying an eager-to-please, frightfully optimistic lad whose misfortune it was to believe the Horatio Alger legend. He was open, cheerful, optimistic, and it is no wonder that he was so well-loved in an America that believed, as never before or since, in the success ethic which motivated his character—and which he gently satirized.

Lloyd himself was a devoted Shriner and an exemplary member of the middle-class community. Of all his contemporaries, he was the only one who simply quit the screen when sound came in, passing his premature retirement in pleasant and profitable non-theatrical pursuits.

In his time he had no peer in the construction of a beautiful string of physically perilous sight-gags which left the viewer limp not merely from laughter but from honest fear for the funnyman's safety. And, as *Harold Lloyd's World of Comedy* has lately proved, his appeal is ageless.

Safety Last. *One of the supreme moments of silent comedy.*

THE MARX BROTHERS

COMEDY DID NOT DIE when the screen began to talk. Rather, certain marvelous comedians found that either they could not talk successfully or that talking deflected the trajectory of their humor, preventing it from reaching the hysteric heights it had once obtained. In due course, screen humor would become almost exclusively a matter of situation comedies, some of them quite good, but all of them the product of ensemble playing by comic actors, rather than the highly individualistic work of pure comedians. Before this happened, however, screen comedy was to be graced by a group of magnificent anarchists called the Marx Brothers and a nonpareil known as W. C. Fields.

The Marxes had been invented by their mother, Minnie, and had straggled up from the lower echelons of vaudeville to the Broadway stage. They came to Hollywood, shortly after the coming of sound, to re-create their stage hits, two of which, *Animal Crackers* and *Duck Soup*, proved to be delicious screen fare. They stayed on to make a succession of movies which, if never totally satisfying, invariably contained sequences of lovely, awesome madness.

The root of Marxism lay in the conflict of the Brothers with their setting. They appeared always as interlopers in a place of power or, at least, high fashion (at a house party; in the cabinet of a mythical kingdom of which Groucho was inexplicably the prime minister; at the opera; at a Saratoga-like spa). Once established, they immediately started to destroy their milieu. Theirs was the maniac humor of nihilism.

They were natural men, unhindered by those notions of good taste and proper behavior which so inhibit the world of the bourgeoisie. Immediately upon arrival, Groucho would establish (a) that he wished to steal a great deal of money by means of a complex confidence scheme; and (b) his love-hate relationship with Grande Dame Margaret Dumont. His technique for interpersonal relations was always

The Marx Brothers Go West, *the hard way of course. As Harpo provides a bridge between cars, he and his brothers provided a bridge between silent comedy and the new style required by sound.*

Three Wise Fools *was the apt title of this late Marx Brothers jape.*

the same—insult upon insult. The upshot was a characterization in which hatred for the conventional was so immense that he could not forbear his insults even if they placed his economic goals in jeopardy.

Groucho stood at the center of the Marxian plot; it was he who set all the wheels to spinning madly. His brothers worked a series of inventive variations on the basic melodic line he established. Periodically a comely blonde, in a state of dishabille, would scamper through, Harpo, horn tooting madly, tiny eyes aglitter, in hot pursuit. His silence disguised the fact that he was completely amoral. Outside, his relationship to the great scheme of things unclear, was Chico in his pointy hat, his Italian accent a bar to the world

of fashion, busily pursuing a more modest form of crookedness than Groucho's. Unlike Groucho, he hid his aggressions and, in the end, displayed more shrewdness than the self-proclaimed mastermind. Usually, in desperation, Groucho would have to enlist Chico's aid to make things come out all right. The end always came suddenly in a Marx Brothers movie—as if they suddenly tired of it and decided to end the nonsense as quickly as possible.

As a team, they were the perfect bridge between silent comedy and sound. Harpo, of course, was the last of the great pantomimists, his special forte being direct action. In a moment of peril he could be relied upon to bring forth from his capacious coat pockets some tool or gadget with

106

which to save the day—a pair of scissors, say, for cutting the phone line over which his enemies were relaying their plans. Groucho was, conversely, among the first of the fast-talking masters of insult, setting a style that was to be the accepted standard among the radio comics of the thirties and forties. Chico, of course, was a dialect comedian familiar to the vaudeville of a slightly earlier time.

Between them, the Marx Brothers represented all the great American comedy styles. Together they transcended all style to answer a felt national need—the utter denigration of upper-class values, values which were widely believed to have caused all the troubles of the decade in which the Marx Brothers achieved their great popularity.

Groucho and Margaret Dumont, in a moment typical of their love-hate relationship.
Miss Dumont, for whom one critic proposed a monument for her unflinching service to comedy, was absolutely essential to a classic Marx Brothers comedy. Indeed, she was practically a member of the family.

W. C. FIELDS

THORSTEIN VEBLEN ONCE DEFINED the chief motivations of the small American businessman as "self-help and cupidity." No one more perfectly portrayed this character than W. C. Fields. Prickly guardian of a few pitiful possessions (the contents of a moribund grocery or drugstore, a sad automobile of uncertain vintage, a flat barely evading classification as a slum), sour protector of the virtue of a family unit which he loathes and which unmercifully deflates his every attempt at dignity, nourisher of some hopeless dream of power and wealth, endless inventor of a past infinitely more appealing than the present, Fields was, par excellence, the *lumpen bourgeois* at bay. One was always certain that, just off screen, the minions of the chain stores were constructing a supermarket that would reduce him to penury.

His scratchy drawl, speaking the pompous clichés which were his sole defense against the intrusive world, was the essence of the man, whining, cajoling, offering empty

W. C. Fields and Mae West, who, off screen, found him rather vulgar, in one of the screen's great confrontations. The film is, of course, My Little Chickadee, *Fields' last truly memorable screen portrayal. Right, as he appeared in* If I Had a Million.

There is some confusion about hats, but not about common goals.

threats against his enemies, most of whom—and this is the cream of the Fieldsian jest—were scarcely aware of his bulbous existence. If only they would pay heed to him, even as they flattened him, he might have been able to bear his fate. Alas, their eyes were on the stars and his were fixed firmly on the petty discomforts of existence.

Fields had to wait for a means to be found to reproduce that inimitable voice of his and so, although a stage star of great repute he did not come to movies until they began to talk. Happily, that coincided with the opening of a great rent in the American dream. At last the world was ready to hear his peculiar version of the frustrations, anxieties, nightmares, crotchets and desperations of those members of the lower orders who insisted on having big-time (or Republican) beliefs on small-time, small town (or Democratic) budgets.

Because of the lamentable gap between his dreams and his reality, Fields was possessed of an abiding, simmering anger which, since he was powerless to vent it on his true tormentors, he turned against small children, cripples, idiots and others so low in life as to be beneath his paltry station. Toward his legion of superiors he turned a face that was both anxiously obsequious and incurably sly. Even as he smiled his false smile and rubbed together his hammy hands,

he was, you could see, planning some small meanness, some sad confidence trick which he knew to be insignificant as protest but which he felt compelled to place on the record.

All of this sprang from the depths of Fields' own being. His childhood, like that of so many great comics, was one of almost unbearable hardship, and he himself suffered the slings of the mighty and the petty wretchednesses of their small-minded fellow-travelers, the cops, clerks and cretins who plague all whose dreams exceed their purses and their powers. He passed his life, even at the height of his fame, in constant warfare with them.

Like the Marx Brothers, Fields never once attempted to enlist our sympathy. He remained a cruel comedian, undoubtedly sensing that, as his excellent biographer, Robert Lewis Taylor, notes, "Most people harbor a secret affection for anyone with a low opinion of humanity." A man's man and a man's comedian, his style owed much to the atmosphere of the barrooms and pool halls, which were the natural habitat—and last refuge—of the marginal man he portrayed. As they have disappeared from the land, so has appreciation for the humor of W. C. Fields, who in a glorious final outburst of the American screen comedian's art, held a wickedly distorting mirror up to a comically dreadful aspect of life.

110

THE MOUSE

Gulliver Mickey.

IN 1938, WHEN THE AESTHETICIANS of the film had gathered Walt Disney and his animated anthropomorphs to their bosoms, a critic wrote: "If Charlie Chaplin's pathetic 'little guy' was the symbol of the last 20 years of social confusion, Walt Disney's animated fables may well supply the key to our progress during the next 20 years." How right he was! Given the prevailing aesthetic of movies, that motion was more important than drama or character (a fundamentally anti-humanist notion), Mickey and friends were the answer to a prayer. Easily integrating color and sound (two factors widely believed to be anti-cinematic) into work in which pantomime remained supreme and dialogue minimal, Disney was regarded as a movie craftsman the equal of Griffith or Eisenstein. Mickey, optimistic, a direct-actionist who opposed violence with violence, fighting bravely for self and ideals in a way heartily approved by a leftist-oriented nation, was more popular than any living comedian of the time. His creator gave out interviews extolling the virtues of experiment and decrying commercialism.

Alas for hopes and ideals! Disney became big business, his Mouse shrank in importance as the studio bent its best efforts to the elaborate and curiously flat feature-length retellings of popular childhood stories (*Snow White, Pinocchio,*

Bambi), then to the quasi-educational true-life adventures, finally to those dismal live-action comedies to which the entire family may safely repair.

The end of the Disney road, a promising one when it began in 1928, is Disneyland, that sterilized carnival which, lacking the lusty amusements of the old-fashioned midway, pretends educational value in order to painlessly extract money from parents gripped by the sentimental notion that education (and reality) must be sugar-coated for the child's benefit. The first Disney cartoons would today be judged too violent for young eyes. Intended as a reflection of a world in a state of upheaval, their exuberant ferocity reflected a delightfully savage comedic sense not unlike that demonstrated in some of the more popular childhood games.

When Disney ceased to appeal directly to the child's innocent love of violent action (and thereby to the child in all of us) and started pandering to the adult's notions of what a child *should* like, he lost his claim to an artist's stature. The trouble was that in the first flush of his enormous popularity he swept all comic competition before him and became the sole trustee of the low-comedy tradition. It is this which he sold out in the children's market—bringing to an end a great, but short-lived, screen tradition.

111

THE

PART FOUR

THIRTIES

SOUND WAS INTRODUCED to the movies in 1927, not in features but in a series of newsreels and short subjects. Its first great success was in a film about Lindbergh's return to America after his historic flight. Despite the great box-office appeal of this little picture, the important studios continued to regard sound merely as an interesting novelty. One or two of them experimented with musical accompaniment and sound effects in their superproductions (*The Big Parade* and *Wings* were among them), but it remained for a minor studio, Warner Brothers, to take the big gamble. They produced *The Jazz Singer*, basically a silent film in which, from time to time, Al Jolson opened his mouth to sing and, lo, song seemed to issue from his mouth.

It was an almost insufferable movie, the sentimental story of a cantor's son from New York's Lower East Side who refuses to follow in his father's footsteps and insists on becoming a musical-comedy singer on Broadway. People came, they listened, and they were conquered. Warner's quickly followed with an *all*-talking film, *Lights of New York*, another banal musical, in which, in its first crude form, that long-term staple, the backstage story of the kid waiting for the first break, had its trial run. The studio's next effort, *The Terror*, dispensed with the main title and credits; Mr. Conrad Nagel, of the gorgeous voice, decked out in mask and opera cape, delivered this information to the audience.

By 1929 *Variety* was reporting that "sound didn't do any more to the industry than turn it upside down, shake the entire bag of tricks from its pocket and advance Warner Brothers from the last place to first in the league." Sound

was, in short, a total revolution—it changed the techniques of making films, radically altered their content, changed the nature of the typical star personality and altered the financial balance of power in Hollywood.

As to technique, the most important immediate effect of the revolution was regressive. The camera, which had grown progressively freer since the days when Griffith first liberated it, suddenly became static, a merely passive observer and recorder of action. Since its whirrings could be picked up by the microphone, it had to be enclosed in a soundproof booth, which effectively immobilized it. Temporarily it became necessary to use as many as three cameras to give the director and editor a variety of shots to which the sound track could later be synchronized. The suddenly cumbersome camera simply could not be moved. In the first two years of sound it was recording virtually nothing of interest anyway. The movies tended to be either closet dramas with no scope and less interest than a stage play, or huge musicals in which Rockette-style choreography was featured as a kind of accompaniment to the blaring sound track.

From film critics and scholars there arose a terrible clamor. The movies, they cried, were finished as an art form, and it is certainly true that the carefully composed aesthetic of the silent film was suddenly in need of amendment. It had been based on the fact that, like all the fine arts, the movies inherently lacked one of the dimensions of total reality. The theory was that in this art, as in painting, music and poetry, the lack, far from being a handicap, was actually a useful limitation, imposing on the artist an artificial barrier which,

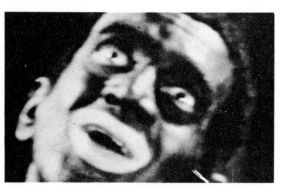

A new era begins: Al Jolson cried out for Mammy and an entire nation cried out for sound.

through illusion, he had to render insignificant. The best silent films (most of which were not made in America) did, indeed, by their concentration on imagery and movement, achieve great force by the strength with which they worked within the limits of the sound barrier. They had a poetry all their own and, for the initiate, a special kind of magic, not unlike that which abstract expressionism has for its followers today.

But, to be realistic about it, silence encouraged in the commercial film medium a kind of banal and overlush romanticism which was neither artistically good nor socially useful. The American films of the twenties—always excepting the comedies—were trash on the lowest possible level. In the thirties films, thanks to sound, became trash on a somewhat higher level. They were prey, it is true, to propagandists who, however sincere their beliefs, managed to muck up, with their busy rakes, some potentially amusing films. If you believe, as this writer emphatically does not, that the movie version of life has a deleterious effect on the impressionable, then you could say that sound films represented a much more internal—and therefore more effective—misrepresentation of reality than did silent movies. They had an insidious feeling of reality about them, but not, on close examination, the ring of truth.

On the other hand, they had certain distinct advantages. Once the initial outburst of banal musicals and dreary soap operas (which seemed always to star Constance Bennett) had somewhat subsided, interesting new genres began to appear. First and foremost, there were the crime films, studies in corrupt power that, by analogy, made strong statements about flaws in the structure of American society. There were films that, at long last, dared to tackle social problems and which, however oversimplified their messages, however naïve they may seem to us today, represented a new seriousness

in movies. The same may be said of the biographical films (frequently starring Paul Muni) and the generally ill-starred efforts to translate literary masterpieces to the screen. The medium, finally, had the technical means, if not the required skills, to adapt from the form it most closely resembles—the novel.

The efforts to use sound with greater subtlety, to use it not merely as a novelty but as a force for greater reality in pictures, bore scattered early fruit—in Lewis Milestone's *All Quiet on the Western Front* (1930), in William Wellman's savage *Public Enemy* (1931), in *I Am a Fugitive from a Chain Gang* (1932), not to mention the sophisticated comedies of Ernst Lubitsch. These films helped free Hollywood from the sudden tyranny of the sound technicians, whose overriding concern was good recording with their crude equipment, and who had briefly supplanted the director as the most important man on the set. The result had been fearful cinematic stasis, a boredom to the eye; even the miracle of sound could not compensate for it.

The better directors soon developed techniques to circumvent the dictatorial microphone men. One was an insistence, in the face of front-office skepticism, that the audience did not have to hear every sound of life, every footstep, every distracting background noise. Their fight was not unlike that of Griffith who had found his backers wary of "foisting half an actor on the public," when he insisted on using close-ups and medium shots in the construction of his films. Directors began shooting action sequences with the mobile silent camera, then dubbing the sound track later. Others insisted on the use of more microphones and the subsequent mixing of their separate tracks in the laboratory.

All of this had the effect of mobilizing the microphone, the limited range of which had tied the camera to movement no greater than the range of a mike's "hearing." Finally, the sound men themselves improved their equipment and quickly found ways to get the camera out of its isolation booth or padded cell. By 1940 the camera had regained all of its old mobility. The films gained a feeling of reality, an ability to deal with ideas, a greater capacity for subtle characterization.

It is irrelevant to discuss what American movies might have been had not the coming of sound set them firmly on a course toward realism. But this much can be safely stated: the aesthetics of reality are the most simply grasped of all artistic standards. They were about all one could hope the men who control the American motion-picture industry might grasp. The men who worked for the moguls understood this and, working on a production-line basis, managed to produce on the sly a great many strong films—sharp, bitter, unrelenting in their attention to detail. They were not flawless in technique, but, within their formulas, they made cogent cinematic statements about the nature of power in our society. Parenthetically, we can note that almost none of the highly praised, independently produced films of social commentary in our own time show the willingness to pursue questions of human motivation to root social and economic causes that was demonstrated, particularly by Warner Brothers, in the thirties.

Insistence on realism naturally had its effect on the star system. Weeded out immediately were the stars who could not speak at all. Recruited posthaste were stage actors who were widely believed to be able to speak beautifully. They, for the most part, did not succeed as well as the average kind of people who spoke—and behaved—with idiomatic naturalness. Sound was not as hard on silent film actors as the new

naturalistic style, as the career of John Gilbert indicates. Ramon Novarro, a second-string romancer of the silents, has said, "I was always the hero—with no vices—reciting practically the same lines to the leading lady. . . . The current crop of movie heroes are less handicapped than the old ones. They are more human. The leading men of silent films were always Adonises and Apollos . . . Today the hero can even take a poke at the leading lady. In my time, a hero who hit the girl just once would have been out. . . ."

The girls who were getting knocked around were a new breed, too. They were no longer virgin princesses but shopgirls, kept women, even prostitutes. They were frequently hard, mannish in dress and behavior, likely to have extremely realistic notions of their lot in life and of the society they inhabited. In short, once Hollywood had sorted out the implications of both the social revolution proceeding outside the studio gates and the technical revolution inside, it found that its stars must now walk among men.

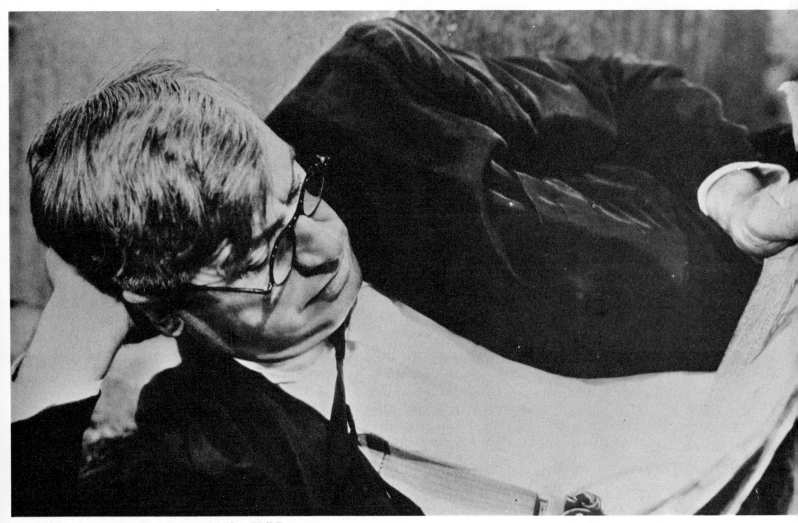

Man of the people: The film success of folksy Will Rogers could not have happened in the romantic silent era.

MAE WEST *New deal for sex*

The face that launched a thousand protests.

ONE DAY IN 1932 Miss Mae West entered a night club, owned, for the purpose of a film script called *Night After Night,* by George Raft. She walked in her inimitable way across the foyer, casting a shrewdly appraising yet somehow humorous gaze over the scene, then wriggled past the hat-check girl. "Goodness, what beautiful diamonds," said that lady, unknowingly participating in an immortal moment in film history. "Goodness," replied Miss West, "had nothing to do with it, dearie." As the laughter built and built, Miss West proceeded to mount a set of stairs, a simple, everyday act which, when performed by the biggest blonde of them all, was a study in the vulgar poetry of motion.

For the rest of the decade Miss West, an aging ex-

vaudevillian, ex-Shubert star, sometime *litterateuse* (she wrote her own plays and often her own movie dialogue), was the screen's leading sex symbol. By 1936 she was being paid the second-highest salary in the United States. Only William Randolph Hearst, who didn't like her, made more.

Mr. Hearst's opinion was shared by other moralists, and there is no doubt that Miss West's presence on the screen was an offense to a noisy minority—principally because she seemed to have so much fun being sexy. This attitude reverses a basic tenet of American popular art which holds that while sex may be discussed in excruciating detail the tone of the talk must be serious, if not quasi-tragic. It is no matter for boffo laughter, although sniggering at "cute" (i.e., suggestive, and therefore dishonest) bedroom farces may in certain circumstances be deemed acceptable.

In any case, Miss West had a ball, as did most of her audience. It is said that her bawdy, straightforward approach to sex comedy was one of the chief reasons for the enactment, in 1933, of the Motion Picture Producers Association Code. For the first time, the Hays office seriously—and successfully—attempted to regulate the content of films, excluding from them certain subjects (e.g., narcotics, sexual deviation), requiring the punishment of all transgressions of accepted moral standards and specifically legislating against all kinds of words, situations and suggestions (exposure of the inside of the female thigh, for instance, was *verboten*). Hollywood, by this time, was feeling the depression, which had not in its early years affected the sale of tickets. In the economic depths, however, people had finally begun to stay away from the dream palaces, and the threat of economic reprisal by moral-uplift pressure groups seriously frightened the industry, the moral tone of which generally follows the business cycle very closely.

But if Mae West was a prime cause of the code, she also saved her studio, Paramount, from bankruptcy. Her producer, William LeBaron, testified: "In the middle of the depression, the Mae West pictures, *She Done Him Wrong* and *I'm No Angel,* broke box-office records all over the country and all over the world. . . . *She Done Him Wrong* must be credited with having saved Paramount Studios at a time when the studio was considering selling out to M-G-M, and

Miss West doing exactly what everyone was afraid of—teaching the young.

when Paramount theaters—seventeen hundred of them—thought of closing their doors and converting their theaters into office buildings."

Basically, the appeal of Miss West was to reason. She took a sensibly mocking attitude toward our attitudes, both romantic and repressive, about sex. She was utterly free of cant, living testimony that it was possible for a woman to have the same sexual needs and desires as a man. The humor came from the fact that she set about satisfying them with the same directness shown by a male on the prowl. In addition, she was a parody mother, a parody showgirl and a parody Grande Dame. She was never, never so vulgar as to

bump or grind. She merely implied these activities with a roll of the eyes, an intonation of her drawling voice.

"No doubt," says the recondite Tyler Parker, "she observed the female impersonator and, spontaneously imitating him, extracted for herself all his comedy, leaving him his pathos. In effect, she expunged the *burlesque* quality from his active masquerade of the female sex." Scott Fitzgerald thought that of all the Hollywood stars she was "the only type with an ironic edge, a comic spark." And Hugh Walpole suggested that "only Charlie Chaplin and Mae West . . . dare to directly attack with their mockery the fraying morals and manners of a dreary world."

Dick Powell, Ruby Keeler and friends in an early Hollywood attempt at neorealism, Flirtation Walk, *1934.*

The Juvenile grown up, as tough Johnny O'Clock, 1947.

DICK POWELL
New deal for song

In 1944, when Dick Powell suddenly appeared as the screen incarnation of Philip Marlowe, Raymond Chandler's hard-boiled private eye, his performance exuded mature masculinity and a tired, semicynical awareness of the perils of life in the urban jungle. It was a startling portrayal, for Powell had come to the screen as a blandly boyish singer, pleasing enough when teamed with dancer Ruby Keeler in silly musicals but hardly the man to administer or absorb a beating from Mike Mazurki.

The essence of Dick Powell had been that of the good-natured, slightly impractical Middle Western boy (which he was in real life) struggling to advance himself in show biz. He was usually discovered in an early reel pounding away at an upright piano, writing and singing unpublishable songs. By the end of the film, someone had propelled him—and Miss Keeler—to the top, he remaining a somewhat befuddled bystander at his own creation as a star.

The virtue of his work was that it was unobtrusive, never interfering with the spectacle of hundreds of girls tap-dancing in unison. His skills as chief executive of his own career were demonstrated by his ability to endure years of this nonsense without failing in public esteem and by his shrewd switch to tough-guy roles at just the right time. From his second career much has followed, including presidency of his own TV production company—one of the busiest in Hollywood—and a TV series which he hosts.

119

Little Caesar before his rise to power . . .

Crime as business

WARSHOW ON THE GANGSTER: "[He] is doomed because he is under the obligation to succeed, not because the means he employs are unlawful. In the deeper layers of the modern consciousness, *all* means are unlawful, every attempt to succeed is an act of aggression, leaving one alone and guilty and defenseless among enemies: one is *punished* for success. This is our intolerable dilemma: that failure is a kind of death and success is evil and dangerous. . . . The effect of the gangster film is to embody this dilemma in the person of the gangster and resolve it by his death. . . . it is *his* death, not ours. We are safe. . . ."

Edward G. Robinson emphasized practical, cold-cash reasons for his depredations. For him, the machine gun represented the extension of the business ethic by other means. For him, as for James Cagney, women were generally irrelevant, though one or two usually skulked close at hand, should biological urgency assert itself. So single-mindedly did he pursue success that he had no time for the niceties of courtship or even ordinary friendship.

Robinson and his great contemporary, Cagney, were prototypical; there had been no one quite like them on the screen before. They were not, precisely, imitations of anything in life, but their manner and behavior quickly became symbols of, and for, a new irreverence for the world of convention and the world of power. They were also symbolic of Hollywood's new view of what the public wanted. It still wasn't utter realism, but the gangster films did present an artistically heightened version of reality. They had a style, a tone of voice—shrill, nasty, and metallically hard—which fitted the national mood.

and after. The politician with whom he is making an alliance is Sidney Blackmer. The year is 1930.

JAMES CAGNEY
Efficiency expert

THE CRIME FILM, says Kenneth Tynan, "has always been openly unreal in structure, depending for its excitement on jazzed dialogue and overstated photography. But its influence on scripting and camera work has been incalculable, involving many of the most expert and adult intelligences in Hollywood. . . . A great deal of desperate urgency and attack would have been lost to the cinema if the gang film had not arrived, making fantastic technical demands. . . ."

The true master of the form was James Cagney, an ex-hoofer who achieved stardom in his first picture, *Public Enemy*, in 1931. Cagney's style was a compound of the dancer's grace, the hustler's energy and an infinite capacity for self-amusement. This amusement took the form of a sadism that carried no sexual charge. It had none of the heavy-breathing gravity of its Teutonic forms. Cagney merely bounded into a scene, chortled merrily and bumped someone off. He did not prolong the moment in order to savor it. He was speedy, efficient, and like the good professional he was, he seemed to enjoy his own skill more than he did its end result.

The traditional conceit of his films was that he was attempting to construct a criminal empire, to realize in his peculiarly American way the peculiarly American dream of the poor boy rising to a position of eminence. But this aspect of his activities was always the least well realized portion of his movies. Like any real artist, the Cagney gangster was more deeply involved in techniques than in such mundane end products as riches, fame, power or women. These last he treated with guarded indifference, and it was implicit in his first crime picture, and painfully explicit in his last (the admirable *White Heat* of 1949), that his best friend, and real love, was his mother. Only if he achieved success in her eyes would he be able, at last, to rest on his Tommy gun.

In the end it is fair to say that Cagney's crook was the first existential anti-hero of the American films. Totally lacking in ideals, supremely contemptuous of conventional morality, he was interested only in the destruction of the world he never made. In every sense he was the man alone, responding to the world's absurdity with a deadly and magnificent display of chillingly humorous destructiveness.

Cagney brought his wondrous energy to the role of George M. Cohan in Yankee Doodle Dandy *and won an Academy Award.*

The bouncy amoralist of the early days.
Left, he invades the privacy of Joan Blondell
in Larceny Love. Below, the Public Enemy
suffers a purely temporary setback, which does
not seem to unduly upset him. The 1931 film
was his first, and he never made a better one.

JEAN HARLOW
New girl in town

JEAN HARLOW PROVIDED the feminine counterpoint to the staccato chatter of the machine gun. Her face was as hard as that of a porcelain doll. Her settings were always high-key, brilliant. There were many mirrors, much white satin, both on her person and in her bedroom, to which the camera quickly repaired and where it lingered long. Her principal occupation was the painstaking application of make-up—a make-up of such high gloss that one could almost catch a reflection in it. The platinum in her hair seemed the result of electroplating, not dye. In her way, she was as frank about sex as Mae West, but with considerable difference—symbolized by their figures. West seemed soft and yielding, a kind of painted earth mother for whom pleasure was everything. Miss Harlow's body was trim and efficient; no doubt she would prove highly efficient in her love making, but there was no promise of a comforting and comfortable afterglow with her. Instead, the implication was that the final act of love's drama would be the exchange of money.

In the movies, the sex queen, the Theda Bara, the Mae West, the Harlow, the Marilyn Monroe—even the Garbo—always ends up playing a parody of herself. It is as if the audience cannot stand for long this physical manifestation of its dream life. It must at a certain point relieve the inner tension engendered by such stars through laughter. With considerable relief, the critics burst into print with the information that the Symbol has become an extremely talented comedienne. Harlow was such when she died in 1937, having refused, because of her Christian Science faith, medical aid for complications following uremic poisoning.

It is also true that stars who symbolize an era's sexual longings rarely find sexual happiness themselves. Harlow's only marriage ended in a month, with her husband's suicide. He, it developed, had been unable physically to satisfy any woman. Only William Powell brought her any happiness. For many years after she died he saw to it that fresh flowers were always present at her grave.

The beautician's delight: Jean Harlow's dress was too tight for her to sit down between takes of Dinner at Eight. *A characteristic preoccupation demands attention in* Blonde Bombshell (right).

and WILLIAM POWELL

To begin with, William Powell was not The Thin Man. The Thin Man was a mysterious stranger who held the key to the mystery in the first film of the series in 1934. Through the years M-G-M tried vainly to explain this nice distinction to the fans of Nick and Nora Charles, but finally gave up, and Powell, who was many things, but never exactly slender, was forever identified as a character he was not.

Otherwise, *The Thin Man* series was a resounding success, providing Americans with a new—and not unhealthy—conception of the perfect marriage. The idea of turning Dashiell Hammett's comic detective story into a movie was exclusively that of W. S. (Woody) Van Dyke, long-term Hollywood character, a director with an unerring ability to turn out any kind of film, under any conditions, on time and under budget. Known as "One Take" Van Dyke, he was a valuable craftsman. Unhindered by temperament or artistic pretensions, he made, within the severe limits of the commercial formula, any number of first-rate films. Among the critics, only Manny Farber has paid tribute to those unsung directors—Howard Hawks, William Wellman, William Keighley, Anthony Mann, Val Lewton—who created the "underground" film. This was the ordinary little picture made solely to meet the need for a steady flow of film into the theaters, to which, so long as it did not slow down the production line, the front office paid no censorious heed. Their creators stressed fast action, snappy dialogue, clean-cut, unfancy film making and, in the process, achieved not only freedom of expression but a uniquely American-type movie. *The Thin Man* was a film in this category and, at his best, Woody Van Dyke was an outstanding underground operative.

He found Hammett's book lying around unused in the story department and bludgeoned the front office into letting him make it on a B-picture budget and schedule (sixteen days). More important, he talked the studio into letting him try Powell and Myrna Loy in the leading roles. Both had been in movies for some time—Powell, an undefined sophisticate, was then making the Philo Vance detective series at another studio; Miss Loy was shuttling between parts as an Oriental siren and as a domestic bad girl.

Together they created an image of *mariage à la mode* which many couples, all unknowing, are still imitating. Independently wealthy, Nick Charles affected a kind of mocking indolence, tended to drink too much and sometimes, in his amiable pursuit of clues, to lose sight of the forest for the trees. He did the big thinking for the pair, but Nora had a shrewd eye for the telling detail and a deliciously wifely way of bringing him down to earth. Nick treated her with indulgent whimsy, pretending to think of her as a scatterbrain, a mannerism which both seemed to know was a necessary indulgence of his male vanity.

Theirs was the best cinematic representation of the workings of the modern male and female intelligences, how they clash and how they mesh. In the context of detection these qualities were thrown into high relief, and the wit and style of the films, though glossier than life, made them enormously entertaining figures in a depression-plagued world that was particularly hard on the institution of marriage. Nick and Nora reassured us that cohabitation can be fun.

The Thin Man. *Left, Nick and Nora Charles engaged in favorite occupations; he is drinking, she is making a wisecrack. Above, a phony but useful faint.*

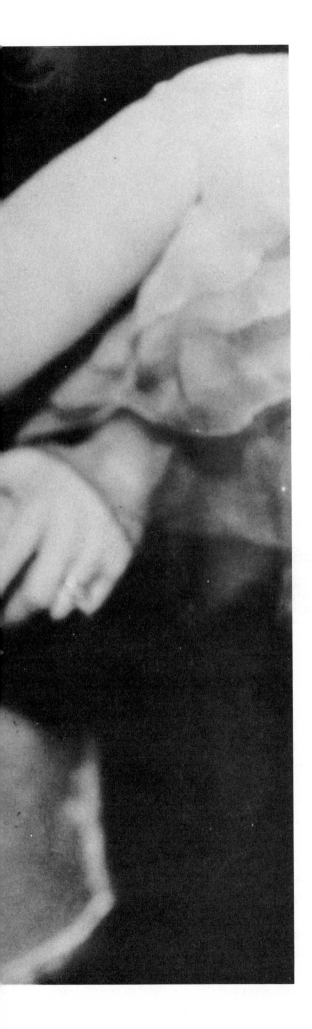

DIETRICH

Temptation without temperament

"THE KRAUT'S THE BEST that ever came into the ring," Ernest Hemingway once told Lillian Ross, and on another occasion he declared, "If she had nothing more than her voice, she could break your heart with it. But she also has that beautiful body and the timeless loveliness of her face."

Marlene Dietrich has become, in our time, the embodiment of a legend. It is a legend of longevity, of glamour retained against the enemy time. But that legend is only the successor to a previous one, which was as a latter-day vamp. Early in her American career C. H. Rand wrote, "Your Latin or Slav vamps of the Pola Negri type don't happen to interest me. I want beauty without bust-ups; temptation without temperament. I want a woman whose passion is not a blind rage of the body or soul, but a recognition of mutual attraction in which reason or humour will play their part, as far as love permits. . . . I find all my requisites in the screen character of Marlene Dietrich."

Miss Dietrich dispensed with the edge of hysteria that was customary in the standard vamp performance and replaced it with a directness, an honesty in her approach to sex that was totally in keeping with the new American taste in these matters. She retained, however, an aura of what the popular press terms "mystery." Almost any actress who speaks from the American screen in a foreign accent will automatically be invested with this quality. Hers was perhaps more genuine than most. She combined, in appearance and in her oddly masculine voice, both command and invitation, and in this there was, indeed, an unsettling quality that, for want of a better term, could be called mystery.

There was nothing mysterious about Marlene Dietrich's past. She was the daughter of a German army officer and she went on the stage in Berlin shortly after the First World War. She played, for the most part, women of unconventional morality, and the famous legs were exploited almost from the start. She worked both in films and on the stage, in musicals

and in straight dramas, but it took Josef Von Sternberg to make an international star of her.

He was a director who had worked both on the Continent and in Hollywood, a great pictorialist, a creator of moods, but not a man with any great sense of pace or dramatic urgency. In 1929 he returned to Germany with Emil Jannings, the great character actor whose career in Hollywood had begun to fail, to make *The Blue Angel.* When Von Sternberg saw Dietrich on stage he knew he had found the perfect foil for Jannings. She was to play Lola, for whose love Jannings would unmercifully degrade himself.

On the basis of her performance, Von Sternberg sold Dietrich to Hollywood and she, who has called him "the man I wanted to please most," insisted on him as her director even though, in time, his humorless style almost ruined her career. He was particularly fascinated by those women who inhabit the twilight zone between the upper levels of whoredom and the lower levels of show business, and most of the films he made with her explored the cruel materialism of the type, the empty sadism they displayed toward their lovers, the total mercilessness of their self-interest. The pictures would have been laughable had it not been for the suggestion of compassion with which Dietrich edged her performances. Even so, she was wise to leave Von Sternberg to make first the witty, highly styled *Desire,* and then *Destry Rides Again.*

She has never totally escaped the milieu of the Von Sternberg films; she is still, more often than not, cast as an entertainer of some sort. We have come to see this as her natural habitat, a feeling she has exploited in her own successful appearances in the clubs in recent years.

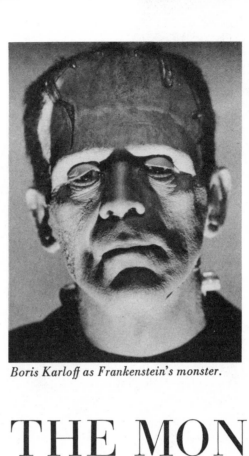

Boris Karloff as Frankenstein's monster.

THE MONSTERS

AFTER LON CHANEY'S DEATH in 1930—artificial snow, made out of cornflakes, lodged in his throat during filming and quickly created a fatal infection—his director, Tod Browning, a master of the grotesque, abandoned the naturalism that had marked the Chaney pictures and went in for the supernatural. His *Dracula* (1931) depended for its success on the creation of an internal logic, a monumental suspension of disbelief. Browning achieved this through the creation, by visual means, of an irresistibly eerie mood which the rational mind found itself powerless to resist. James Whale's *Frankenstein* was equally successful and in the monsters the public found symbols expressive of their own situation. The monsters were ghastly, living mistakes, cruel evidence that systems—and men—could fail through no fault of their own. In 1930–31 almost every American could testify, from personal experience, to the truth of this notion.

Lon Chaney, Jr., last of horror's big three as the Wolf Man.

Bela Lugosi has already done his worst to Helen Chandler in Dracula, *first of the horrids.*

133

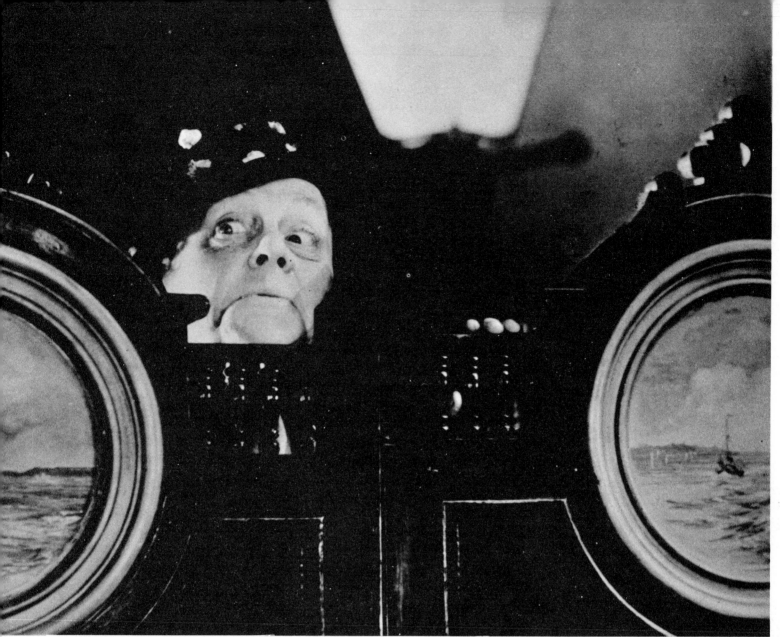

Marie Dressler as the only living thing in the dull and pompous Anna Christie.
the film in which "Garbo Talks!"

MARIE DRESSLER

MARIE DRESSLER, A WOMAN of monumental proportions and presence, had been a star, both in comedy and drama, on the legitimate stage, in vaudeville and in pictures for most of her fifty-eight years when, in 1927, she found herself at the bottom of the deepest trough of her career. Broke, she was rescued by an M-G-M script writer named Frances Marion, who wrote a part into an Irish comedy for Miss Dressler, then persuaded Thalberg to cast her. The film, vehemently protested by sundry Hibernian orders, had to be withdrawn, but Thalberg did not lose faith in Dressler. His patience was well rewarded when, in 1930, the star provided the only vitality in the otherwise static and ludicrous *Anna Christie.* Playing a slatternly dockside doxy, Dressler was an incom-

parable combination of the proud, the self-pitying and the vulgar.

The permanence of her comeback was assured when she teamed with the rude Wallace Beery in *Min and Bill*, a lusty comedy about a frowzy, quarrelsome and sentimental pair of old sots. The film sealed the success of both stars' comebacks and until cancer struck her down Marie Dressler was the highest paid performer at Metro. She earned her position through a simple trick: when playing a woman of wealth, she always added a broad touch of the common; when playing the common she always added a little bit of the grand. She thus attained a kind of universality—certainly a fine comedy of contrast.

134

SHIRLEY TEMPLE

SHIRLEY TEMPLE WAS BORN in Santa Monica, just ten miles from Hollywood, on April 23, 1928. Her father was manager of a bank, and her mother was intelligently ambitious. At three the child began taking dancing lessons, and after her third lesson a scout picked her up for work in a series of short subjects in which babies burlesqued adult films. She did bits in features "just for the fun of it," her mother later said, then got the chance, at age six, to sing one song, "Baby Take a Bow," in *Stand Up and Cheer*. She got a contract on the basis of it, and, for some reason, appeared to every mother in America to be either the girl they had wanted to be, or the girl they wanted their daughters to be. She made seven pictures that year, the last of which billed her alone above the title.

She was in manner a pre-pubescent Mary Pickford—cute, cheerful, dreadful—and all over America mothers got out their curling irons to twist their daughter's hair into the fifty-five curls that always surmounted Shirley's perpetual baby face. No child star before or after Miss Temple achieved so large a cult, so quickly. Undoubtedly she owed her success to the depression, which created a desperate need for her sort of vacuous cheerfulness. Was there more to it than that? Perhaps: let us merely note that she successfully prosecuted a libel suit against Graham Greene after he suggested that she was, in manner, a pocket Claudette Colbert, capable of the same kind of coquetry.

Shirley Temple, in The Little Colonel, *and as Shirley Temple* (above).

MICKEY ROONEY

ALL THE CHILD STARS before Rooney had been insufferably sweet. He was the first to achieve greatness as an out-and-out brat. Since adolescents are ever thus, Rooney achieved a unique rapport with the parents in his audience. They regarded him with much of the exasperated affection they held for their own children. Compared to someone like Shirley Temple, he was tonic. Rooney was the son of a vaudeville family and had been trouping since he was six. He was thirteen when David Selznick found him providing the entertainment for a children's ping-pong tournament and signed him in 1933. His first film was *Broadway to Hollywood* in

which he was type-cast as the son of a vaudeville couple. He played Clark Gable as a boy in *Manhattan Melodrama*, then played the bad-little-boy to the good-little-boy of Freddie Bartholomew in a couple of pictures. Then there was the relationship between Rooney and Spencer Tracy; he played Tracy's son in *Captains Courageous*, Tracy's toughest charge in *Boy's Town*, and even *Young Tom Edison*, the sequel of which was *Edison the Man* starring Tracy. Finally, there were the kid-stuff romances with Judy Garland, the Andy Hardy series and, at last the mature Rooney, now over forty, an energetic and expert character actor whose very presence as an adult reminds us—uncomfortably—of how time flies, which fact prevents him from again attaining the true stardom of his youth.

136

Mickey Rooney was a refreshingly bratty child star, as exasperatingly impossible as your own youngster. Here he is in Babes in Arms, one of those show-bizzy tales in which he costarred with Judy Garland. The film was based on the Broadway hit of Rodgers and Hart, but you had to look awfully hard to find more than a superficial resemblance.

JUDY GARLAND
The edge of peril

A star is reborn: Judy Garland in the 1954 remake of A Star Is Born, *with James Mason. The film was a high point in one of Garland's many recent comeback efforts.*

FRANCES GUMM ALSO BEGAN her career as a professional entertainer at the age of three, in 1927. But, unlike Temple, she was eleven before she came to a studio. She was renamed Judy Garland and, with another child star, named Deanna Durbin, made a little short subject called *Every Sunday.* Corny, brutal, megalomaniacal Louis B. Mayer, head of production at M-G-M, had a weakness for films about kids and families—subjects he regarded as particularly and heart-warmingly American. It was he who made the contracts with Garland and Durbin, he who decided, when the short was finished, that they should be teamed—and he who fairly tore the studio apart when he discovered that the latter had been allowed to escape to Universal.

The mistake very nearly cost Judy her career, for the studio could think of nothing very exciting for her to do. Idling under contract, she got a chance to sing at a studio party, impressing executives enough to let her do a bit in *Broadway Melody of* 1938. She was teamed with Rooney both in and out of the Hardy series and at last was cast as Dorothy in *The Wizard of Oz.* It charmed the nation and created for Miss Garland a sympathy with her public that has withstood the many cruelties of the years since.

Engaged, in 1961–62, in the third major comeback of her career, Miss Garland, like nearly everyone else, was at a loss to find the reason for the magical hold she has on an audience. "It may be my power of concentration," she told writer Jack Hamilton. "I really mean every word of every song I sing, no matter how many times I've sung it before. . . . All you have to do is never cheat and work your best and work your hardest, and they'll respond to you."

She was close to the truth. In general, great performances, especially on film, seem to result from an inner tension, the tension created by raw energy and the performer's control of that energy. At her finest, Miss Garland, especially in her maturity, seems always about to be destroyed by her own inner forces. It puts a quiver of passion in her voice and a chill in the listener's spine. At every moment of a Garland performance you feel that you stand with the star on the brink of disaster, and a hundred times a night she saves herself—and her sympathetic admirers—from the abyss.

Ray Bolger, Jack Haley, Judy, and Bert Lahr "Follow the Yellow Brick Road" in The Wizard of Oz.

FRED ASTAIRE

GARLAND'S GREATNESS is based on the openness with which she draws the audience into the performance. You are supposed to feel what she feels as she works, to sense, if not to fully understand, the psychological pressures that contribute to the force of performance. In the openness with which she has allowed her illnesses of body and spirit to be discussed in public and the contribution this knowledge makes to our understanding of and identification with her public personality, she is very much the child of our time. It being the age of psychology, Garland, partly by choice, partly because of the public's strong desire to invade the celebrity's privacy, has used her weaknesses—and ours—to build an almost fanatical bond of identification between herself and her audience.

Fred Astaire is a performer of exactly the opposite kind. One never sees in his work a gesture which is not perfection. The man's movements have the open grace, the confidence which is the result of concentrated study and lifelong discipline. But, of course, he confides nothing. He is a very private man who personifies stylishness but reveals little of his inner self. Not that the spectator feels any need to ask for more than Astaire gives. There is, indeed, no more satisfying performer in the world.

The dancer's basic tool is the space through which he moves; it is his business to create, out of emptiness, the ordered patterns of art. Astaire's special virtue, as an artist, has been to dominate any space he chooses, with consummate ease. One does not imagine him struggling for this dominance, and the spectator for the most part fails to remember that such ease can result only from the most intense off-stage efforts. This seeming ease is the secret of his appeal. Says film choreographer Hermes Pan: "Fred can dance a very intricate routine, and he makes it look so simple and easy. It gives the audience a sense of self-identification and a feeling that they, too, can do it."

The seams of his work never show, and neither does the intensity of the man who creates it. In fact, nothing shows but what Astaire wants to show, which is casualness, coolness, a taste for relaxed elegance, a shy humor, a modesty which seems to hold his art very lightly—as an unprecious achievement. It is said that he has a fiery temper but that it is directed only at people who attempt to interfere with the integrity of his work or at those who are unprofessional in their attitudes toward dance. "I have never seen such a dedi-

The Sky's the Limit *(1943), contained some of Astaire's greatest dancing.*

The edge of perfection

The beloved partnership: Astaire and Ginger Rogers in Swing Time *(1936).*

cated man," says one film producer. "He rehearses twice as much as any kid just breaking in."

His contribution to the art of the screen is larger than that of almost any other performer, for few can claim to have revamped an entire screen genre. When he came to Hollywood, after years of theatrical stardom with his sister Adele the screen musical was still in its vulgar infancy. Its chief features were what seemed to be hundreds of girls performing the most banal and brassy routines in ludicrous back-

stage, Graustarkian or collegian settings, an awkwardness of technique that was appalling.

Astaire was afraid of Hollywood and what it might do with him, and Hollywood didn't quite know what to make of him. "Can't act. Slightly bald. Can dance a little," read the now famous report on his screen test. He was loaned out for a small part with Joan Crawford in *Dancing Lady*, then began the immensely profitable and pleasurable series of films with Ginger Rogers. The two did not get on well, but, between

The Swinging Partners

First film: The Dancing Lady, *with Crawford.*   You Were Never Lovelier. *Astaire and a favorite partner, Rita Hayworth.*

them, they shifted the style of cinematic dance. No longer did the plot have to be a theatrical one in order to provide a rationale for dancing. They could dance any time, any place, anywhere. When they whirled into motion it seemed merely a natural expression of whatever emotion had seized them.

One always had to stifle a laugh when Nelson Eddy, in the midst of a primeval forest, or a revolution, suddenly burst into song so deafening that you feared for Miss MacDonald's eardrums; it was all so terribly false. There was nothing of that about Astaire and Rogers. His singing was a sort of hoarse whisper, totally without the big mannerisms and tones of the operatic tradition which rang so false in the intimacy of the movies. The same could be said of his non-acting—it was always offhand, natural, gentle even in anger. Almost singlehanded Astaire brought the musical back to earth, fitting it to the pseudo-realistic requirements of the screen. Furthermore, he freed screen dance from the necessity of being a huge spectacle, made of it the expression of an individual. He insisted that the camera stay still, focused on his full figure, shrewdly sensing that he alone could provide all the movement the medium required, that all else would be distracting and irrelevant

The total effect was summed up by Astaire himself one time. "I don't dig this brooding, analytical stuff," he said. "I just dance, and I just act." This, of course, is the impression he has sought to convey through his artless art these many years. He "just" dances, "just" acts, "just" *is*. And perhaps there is no more to Astaire than meets the eye. What meets the eye is, of course, utterly charming, completely amusing, totally distracting.

Astaire and Rogers again (left) *and Astaire and Cyd Charisse* (above), *in* The Bandwagon, *a fine film version of the Schwartz-Dietz revue.*

143

ul Muni in The Good Earth, *film that brought Luise Rainer her second Oscar.*

PAUL MUNI

The disguised hero

ɔLLYWOOD, WITH ITS USUAL imperception, tried to make ʌul Muni into a new Lon Chaney—a man with a thousand ces. Muni, always terribly serious about his work, rebelled this and, as he tells it, literally did handsprings in his ʾing room when he bought out his Warner Brothers contract the late thirties. A shy man who said that "all the things at usually appeal to an actor make me shrivel inside," he ɪdoubtedly found it comforting to hide beneath his sundry, ɪd exceedingly clever, make-ups.

Through most of them, however, shone certain qualities ι which the audience could always depend. Whether he was ʾla, Pasteur, Juarez or a Chinese peasant, he generally ex-ɓited a lovable crustiness, a mildly eccentric nonconformity ιat made his character seem, no matter how remote the time place in which he was set, comfortably familiar to us. the end we perceived beneath the disguise an uncle or grandfather, wise, humorous, patient, given to endearing ʈle outbursts of temper. His great use in the films was to ιke the unfamiliar seem suddenly as recognizable and com-ʈtable as the drama of our own living room.

Muni made a career of playing men older than himself or, at least, ones who aged considerably in the course of the work in hand. As a child and young man he appeared in literally hundreds of the Yiddish theater productions with his family. The first was at the age of twelve, and naturally he played a little old man. His first Broadway success was also as a gaffer, whom he mimed so skillfully that one critic ex-pressed outrage that "this old man should have spent a life-time waiting for a chance to appear on Broadway."

His acting technique was based on an uncanny talent, both physical and vocal, for mimicry and imitation; it is his ex-hausting habit to read and study for months before creating the outer shell of the character in which the unchanging Muni hides. Aided by his wife, he zealously and jealously protects his privacy, and he was careful, in the comparatively brief years of his great success, to build an economic security en-abling him to live a modest life without depending on acting for sustenance. In truth, his considerable art is based on concealment not revelation, and it is unlikely that he ever once exposed any aspect of the real Paul Muni to public gaze.

uni in his first great film success, I Am a Fugitive from a Chain Gang *(1932).*

BETTE DAVIS
The disturbed heroine

ONE OF HER HUSBANDS, Gary Merrill, said that "whatever Bette would have chosen to do in life, she would have had to be the top or she couldn't have endured it." Probably no truer words have ever been spoken about Miss Davis. The question of whether she is really a great actress—in the theatrical, rather than the movie sense—has yet to be settled. But no one has ever been better than Davis at her best on the screen. She had tremendous nervous energy which communicated itself in a hundred small ways—the intensity of her voice, the famous mannerisms with the cigarette, the way in which her huge eyes skittered about, nervous, insecure, trying, it seemed, to discover a lurking peril, which never was far away in a Davis picture. Her responses had an electric intensity that verged on hysteria. One got the impression of a woman teetering along the brink of a breakdown—a breakdown which never came because, in the end, by sheer will, she would pull herself together and, if not avert disaster, learn to live with it or to profit from it.

Miss Davis created a new screen type—the modern woman, neurotic, threatened, uncertain about her role in life, but determined to fight for happiness. Usually, she played a woman of considerable status—either an inheritor of wealth or the possessor of a prosperous career, a little bit mannish in manner, but beneath her aggressive exterior, frightened and lonely. There was a wild quality about this creation; you could never be absolutely certain what she might do next. But a strong man, a man as sure of his masculinity as the Davis character wanted to be sure of her femininity, could tame her.

As for Miss Davis herself, she was—and is—a woman of temperament and determination. Had she not possessed both qualities she would not have been a star at all, for although she had a youthful freshness, she was no beauty in the usual screen sense. Born in Lowell, Massachusetts, April 5, 1908, she was reared in impoverished gentility; educated in private

high schools and after graduation went to New York to study at the John Murray Anderson drama school. After the usual testing period in stock, she got two good parts on Broadway —in *Broken Dishes* and in *The Solid South*. Her first screen contract, with Universal, followed. She recalls that she had "about as much sex appeal as Slim Summerville," and after a succession of dreary roles, she found herself out of a con-

Bette Davis in a role for which she was born, The Virgin Queen.

The first film after her strike against Warner Brothers. She wanted better roles, got one in 1937 gangster film, Marked Woman.

The poor little rich girl of Dark Victory, *1939.*

Dark Victory *again, after the noble doctor (George Brent) has*

tract and ready to go back to New York. Just then, however, George Arliss was searching for a young girl for a small, good part in *The Man Who Played God*. Davis got it and was on her way.

The next major turning point in her career was as the man-killing waitress in *Of Human Bondage*, the first picture in which all of her tremendous power was unleashed. The fresh-faced ingenue returned from time to time, notably in *The Petrified Forest* (1936), but energy and neurosis came more and more to dominate her screen characters, especially after her famous strike against Warner Brothers when she demanded better roles and got them, starting with *Marked Woman* in 1937 and continuing through *Jezebel, Dark Victory, The Old Maid, The Little Foxes, Now, Voyager* and finally that epochal summation of the Davis screen character, *All About Eve*.

In the years since that wonderful film, Miss Davis' career has been in something of a decline. Too honest to attempt to maintain a spurious youthfulness, she looks her age now and is barred by it from playing romantic parts, despite the fact

that many of her contemporaries are still faking youthfulness. Refusing to live for any length of time in Hollywood, the phoniness of which she dislikes, she has tried the theater which has squandered her talent in a way that it usuall criticizes movies for doing.

She herself now affects a certain weariness. "I enjoy acting," she told an interviewer, "but I don't have to do it t be happy. You change through the years and lose somethin along the way. You don't remain as much a fighter as yo get older. Things don't seem as important as they once did.

Many people believe that Miss Davis' well-known desire t have things her own way in pictures proved her prematur undoing. In the late years of her career as the top dramati star of American films she seemed deliberately to insist o actors who were not her equal and directors whom she coul dominate. By 1945 the perceptive James Agee noticed wha was going wrong. Reviewing *The Corn Is Green*, he wrote "It seems to me she is quite limited, which may be no sin b is a pity, and that she is limiting herself beyond her right by becoming more and more set, official and first-ladyish i

shown her the true meaning of life.

mannerism and spirit, which is perhaps a sin as well as a pity. . . . I have a feeling that Miss Davis must have a great deal of trouble finding films which seem appropriate, feasible and worth doing, and I wish that I, or anyone else, could be of use to her in that. For very few people in her position in films mean, or could do, so well. But I doubt that anything could help much unless she were willing to discard much that goes with position—unless, indeed, she realized the absolute necessity of doing so."

This is probably as full and fair a statement of the artistic dilemma in which Miss Davis found herself in the middle and late forties as could be made. An individualist and a potential talent of the first rank, she devoted herself to an industry that loathes the first and pays only lip service to the second. Now, without the position she once had, she seems to be living with the artistic daring she once fought for, then seemed to lose after she achieved the status she also craved. She remains a great lady, one of the very few who dared and succeeded at the grand manner in a movie age that did not appreciate it.

Storm Center, *one of the succession of poor recent films which Davis has illuminated by her presence. In this one she played a librarian fighting to save her books from the censors.*

Leslie Howard as Romeo. Norma Shearer was Juliet in this 1936 try for culture.

LESLIE HOWARD
The perfect Englishman

"I AM," SAID LESLIE HOWARD, "one of those unfortunate people to whom any kind of public appearance is an embarrassment, for whom to have to perform before my fellow men is a misery.... From the moment when, offered accidentally and accepted economically, I got my first job on the stage and sheepishly daubed my face with grease paint, I had the inner conviction that this was the most embarrassing occupation in the world."

This attitude may have been something of a pose, but it is true that Howard was vague, forgetful, shy—and somehow extremely charming. He had the great virtue of being unserious about himself, and in the thirties, when Hollywood was host to scores of English actors whose elegant enunciations of the language were much prized, Howard was the most interesting of a type. His style was ideally suited to movie acting. Even as a stage actor he had demonstrated the knack of infusing each new part with his own personality.

Brooks Atkinson wrote, at the time of Howard's stage triumph in *The Petrified Forest*: "His style of playing is such a lucid expression of his light slender buoyant personal appearance that I confess I am unable to tell how his acting of Alan Squïer differs from his acting of Peter Standish in *Berkeley Square* or Tom Collier in *The Animal Kingdom*. In my mind all those parts are permanently stamped in the image of Mr. Howard's limpid personality."

What was most clear in Howard's work was that he was a shy romantic, an uninsistent cavalier. He was extremely myopic, so his gaze seemed always to be fixed on some far horizon rather than on the mundane present. Hence the performances for which he is best remembered: Alan Squier; Ashley in *Gone with the Wind* (of which he said, "Terrible lot of nonsense—heaven help me if I read the book"); the violinist in *Intermezzo*; even the visionary airplane designer in his last film, *Spitfire*. He was par excellence the dreamer, and his death in 1943, in a commercial plane shot down by Nazi raiders, was an appropriate one. He had been on an unimportant wartime mission, but one which represented the best contribution an actor could make to a cause in which he deeply believed and for which he had willingly, quixotically made sacrifices—including, finally, his life.

The real Howard: myopic, informal, charming.

Howard in Intermezzo. *He played opposite a newcomer named Ingrid Bergman.*

Charles Boyer in Arch of Triumph *(above)* and in his most famous role,
Pepe LeMoko in Algiers *(1938) with, of course, Hedy Lamarr.*

CHARLES BOYER
The perfect Continental

The Romantic. Boyer turns on the charm for Ingrid Bergman's benefit.

JUST AS HOWARD WAS the perfect Englishman, Charles Boyer was the perfect movie Frenchman, ideal symbol of those magically romantic qualities with which Anglo-Saxons have always invested the Gallic male. His deep and vibrant voice spoke a promise of new adventures in love, his deep, sad eyes bespoke a worldly knowledge untarnished by cynicism. He had the boudoir grace of Valentino without the hysteria or the sometime effeminacy of the great lover. Boyer, in short, was an old-style romantic without the grand manner.

He came to Hollywood in the early thirties, was miscast in a series of small parts (he was Jean Harlow's chauffeur in *Red-Headed Woman*), played in the specially prepared French versions of American movies then being filmed on the Coast, finally quit in disgust to return to his fine French career. He came back to play a curly-haired gypsy in *Caravan*, then made his breakthrough in *Private Worlds* (1935), an early psychodrama costarring Claudette Colbert. *Mayerling* and *Algiers* consolidated his position.

After the war, the romantic years past, he established himself once again as a serious actor (on Broadway in *Red Gloves* and *Don Juan in Hell*), as an able *farceur* (*Kind Sir* and *The Marriage-Go-Round*), finally as an excellent movie character man (*Fanny*). A frequently parodied actor, he has had the dignity never to parody his former screen self.

CAROLE LOMBARD
The perfect realist

Nothing Sacred—*not even the jaw Fredric March socks.*

COMEDIENNES WERE THE NEW WAVE of the thirties. What was funny about them was that they always turned out to be more realistic than the men in their pictures. They had a sharper sense of right and wrong, were better students of tactics, and were masters of the mannish wisecrack. In a movie world where women had, prior to the depression, been either innocents or exotics, they were refreshingly down-to-earth. In comedy, previously dominated by males—with women used only as foils or decoration—they actually set the style of the period. For want of a better term, they were known as screwballs and, of them all—Jean Arthur, Rosalind Russell, Claudette Colbert—the best was Carole Lombard.

Born in Indiana, she came to Los Angeles as a child and did her first movie work at age eleven. She waited all of four years before going to work full time in the movies. Junior-high diploma in hand, she reported for work as a cowgirl in Buck Jones Westerns at seventy-five dollars a week, then graduated to Mack Sennett comedies. Joseph P. Kennedy, then heading Pathé, saw her and offered her more money to appear in films at his studio—if she would lose weight. She agreed, but made a splendid exit from his office, crying, "You're not so skinny yourself." He went into training, and Miss Lombard went into bigger and bigger pictures—*Twentieth Century, My Man Godfrey* and, best of all, *Nothing Sacred* (1937), a Ben Hecht joke on newsmen and publicity stunts. Her screen personality was implacably logical—like that of the great comics and all womankind.

Off screen she was a blunt-spoken practical joker, given to such pranks as screwing flash bulbs into light sockets and lingering to wait for the explosion when an innocent turned the light on. She once rewrote a contract with her agent specifying that *he* pay her 10 per cent of her salary. She wooed Clark Gable with a model T on which she pasted hundreds of paper hearts and when they were married became a regular guy, placing his tastes—and career—ahead of her own. She was in all ways a delight, and her death in a wartime plane accident was a genuine tragedy.

Starlet days. Carole Lombard shares a beachball with Diane Ellis.

Fools for Scandal. *Behind one of those masks is Ralph Bellamy.*

HENRY FONDA *The perfect rustic*

IN *The Seesaw Log*, William Gibson tells of a moment in rehearsal when Henry Fonda drew director Arthur Penn aside and told him "that what he had to give the public was naturalness and ease, which this part did not let him feel, and that his nights were sleepless with worry. In all this there was aesthetic and personal honesty. Hank could not bear to deliver a line falsely, just as I never heard him utter a sociable insincerity to any of us . . ."

This comes from a man with whom Fonda had perhaps the most serious artistic disagreements of his career. Both before and after this unhappy experience Fonda demonstrated a shrewd and honest ability to judge the limits of his appealing talent and rarely, if ever, has he overmatched himself; rarely, if ever, has he failed to work strongly within his limits. He came to movies from the stage, where he had scored a hit, after the usual apprenticeships, in *The Farmer Takes a Wife*.

The flat accents of his native Middle West and the direct honesty of his mien stood him in good stead in that bucol[ic] gambol, and although Fonda has demonstrated a flair f[or] farce, he has not lost the accent or its implications in t[he] mythology of our time. It seems to stand for the rustic vi[r] tues—honesty, integrity, sincerity—and whether he is wea[r] ing a six-shooter, a naval officer's uniform or the well-c[ut] attire of a banker, those virtues accompany his presence.

His first movie successes came in dramas of social co[n] sciousness, notably as Tom Joad in *The Grapes of Wra*[th] and as Frank James in *Jesse James*, a message Western [in] which the noted thieves were portrayed as Robin Hoods ai[d] ing poor farmers caught in the toils of rail and banki[ng] interests. There was need for his type in the films of t[he] thirties and he made one of the last and best of the rur[al] social dramas, *Ox-Bow Incident* (1943), an honest, dus[ty] study of lynch law. He now operates mainly in city gar[b] but a little bit of what is best about the life of the la[nd] clings to his presence.

Frank James makes his getaway. The film is Jesse James *(193*[9]

Fonda as Tom Joad in The Grapes of Wrath, *one of the many honest rustics he played.*

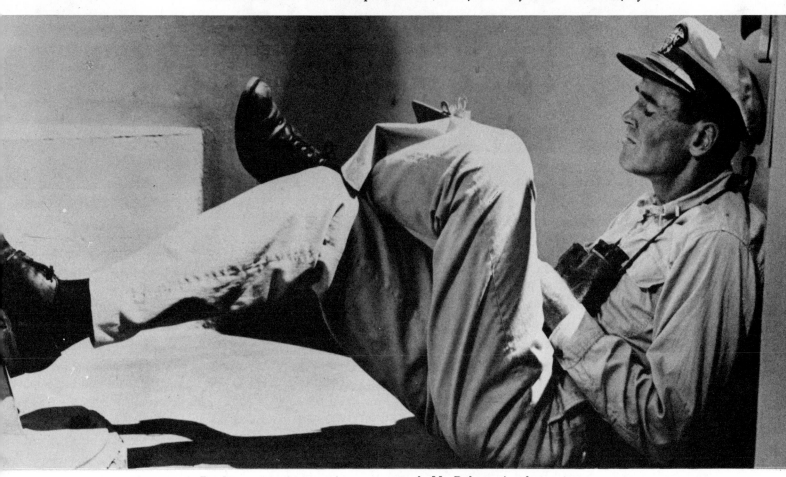

Fonda recreates his most famous stage role, Mr. Roberts, *for the movies.*

CLAUDETTE COLBERT

Virtue is wronged by Edmund Lowe in The Misleading Lady.

"YOU HARLOT," cried Fredric March.

"I love you," simpered Claudette Colbert.

"That's enough," said Cecil B. DeMille.

On the basis of five words of dialogue he decided to turn a pleasant young comedienne into Poppaea, wickedest woman in the world. The justly famed bath in asses' milk in *The Sign of the Cross* (1932) would shortly follow. There were some things that sound and the depression could not change. Among them were the public's love of spectacle, the movies' transcendent ability to provide same, and Cecil B. DeMille's mastery of the form. He would turn, after this film, from rewriting Biblical history to experiments with the American past, until after the Second World War Americans tired of

patriotism and were ready for such religious consolation as he could offer. The DeMille formula did not change whatever the period. It was always a blend of sex, sadism, action, pseudo nobility and, for the individual who abandoned attitudes at the door, great good fun.

As for Miss Colbert, a transplanted Parisian with considerable stage and screen experience prior to the big lift DeMille gave her in *The Sign of the Cross* and in *Cleopatra,* she sensibly varied her pace throughout the decade. The year she made *Cleopatra* she also made *It Happened One Night,* and whether playing the Queen of the Nile or a rich girl on the run, she retained a kind of wide-eyed innocence and youthful gaiety which never grew tiresome.

Virtue defends herself—after a fashion—in The Wiser Sex.

Virtue is wronged by the Puritans in Maid of Salem.

Power and Gene Tierney in Son of Fury *(1942).*

THE BEARER OF A DISTINGUISHED NAME in the annals of stage melodrama, Tyrone Power, Jr., was destined to turn to the movies, inheritor of the audience and many of the basic ideas of the popular theater. In 1937 he dropped the "Jr." from his name, and in the fifties he essayed, with considerable success, some serious dramatic roles on the stage. He died in 1960 while filming *Solomon and Sheba* in Spain.

His first film successes were as an extremely callow juvenile, notably in *Lloyds of London* (1936). He quickly matured, however, into a leading man of the classic type—exuding a kind of generalized sex appeal while suggesting no strongly personal traits. He could thus play any part—Western, urban, comic, dramatic—without becoming automatically typed. Yet, because he was a man of intelligence and some sensitivity, he occasionally rose above being a mere leading man and did a bit of acting, notably in *Nightmare Alley*. He had intelligence, adaptability and energy that other leading men—equally reliable—lacked.

A couple of cons named Lloyd Nolan and Tyrone Power fight it out in Johnny Apollo.

TYRONE POWER

Leading men
ROBERT TAYLOR

*A hero for every age: Above, Taylor appears as Ivanhoe,
and as a cowboy. Left, he is the noblest Roman of
them all, a centurion converted to Christianity in* Quo Vadis?

UNDOUBTEDLY THERE EXISTS, somewhere, the real Robert Taylor, a man with frets, passions, anxieties, humors customarily associated with human existence. That man, or even a hint of him, has yet to appear on any movie screen. No full-scale emotion, not even the suggestion of some engaging quirk of character, has ever been allowed to mar the impressive impassivity of Taylor's remarkably beautiful countenance. He was, in his prime, the male equivalent of the Love Goddess, existing for no purpose but to be worshiped, and it is significant that his first movie success was as Garbo's youthful lover, Armand, in *Camille*, that curious exercise in somnambulism, in which two objects of perfect beauty swam with entrancing unreality before our eyes for an hour and a half. Taylor was then not long out of Pomona

College and only a few films away from his debut in *Broad-way Melody of 1936*, in which for reasons clear only to a movie mogul he warbled "I Got a Feeling You're Foolin'" and danced a little.

After *Camille* he played in everything, finding his metier in such heavy postwar costume epics as *Quo Vadis?* and *Ivanhoe*, where his somewhat remote presence in no way interfered with our appreciation of scenery, costumes, and casts of thousands engaged in a clattering clutter of expensive action. To this day Mr. Taylor has not learned how to speak a line with even rudimentary believability, age (he is now fifty-one) has stained his beauty, but he continues to work, a slightly decrepit god who, naturally shy, has hidden behind the beautiful mask nature so kindly provided him.

Leading men FREDRIC MARCH

WHEN FREDRIC MARCH WAS GRADUATED from the University of Wisconsin he received a scholarship which provided for his training as a banker at the National City Bank of New York. He did not last long in finance, abandoning his apprenticeship for work as a Belasco extra. But he has not lost in the intervening years the dignity and solidity that are usually associated with the money man. A certain sobriety is always present in his performances and is, indeed, a sort of trademark with him. This is not to say that March, particularly in films, is not an actor of considerable range, sensitivity and subtlety. The screen, where much can be indicated by the flicker of an expression, is the medium for which he was born.

He came to Los Angeles in the touring company of *The Royal Family* in 1928, stayed on to play the John Barrymore part in the film version and has since played upwards of sixty film roles. They have ranged from Roman centurions to American admirals, from Philip of Macedonia to Anthony Adverse, from Dr. Jekyll and Mr. Hyde (his first Academy Award performance) to, coming full circle, a humanistic banker in *The Best Years of Our Lives,* for which he won a second Oscar. He has no peer at playing the gruff, middle-class professional man, and it is these portrayals which mark the main line of his film career.

The several faces of Fredric March. Above, he is the grumpy pathologist of The Young Doctors. *Left, he appears in* Christopher Columbus *(1949), a dull film.*

Don't make waves! March carries John Beal through the Paris sewers in Les Misérables.

The carnivore BARBARA STANWYCK

"I want to go on until they have to shoot me," Barbara Stanwyck has said.
With Ronald Reagan, in Cattle Queen of Montana, *she does some shooting of her own.*

NEARLY EVERY WOMAN who achieved movie stardom during the 1930's was called upon, at one time or another, to act tough. The hard woman was a basic discovery of the American movie industry in this period, but of all the brassy or wisecracking or mannish women who disported themselves on the screen in the decade after the movies began to talk, only one woman built a durable career out of toughness. That was Barbara Stanwyck. Her specialty was a narrow-eyed, thin-lipped and totally withering glare combining contempt, avarice and a challenge to humanize her which could fell a male pursuer in his tracks. She was utterly impenetrable and utterly implacable in pursuit of her goals which were (a) money and (b) destruction of the male animal.

Miss Stanwyck's films seldom offered any explanation of why she was so lacking in the ordinary female emotions. She simply existed, hard as nails, the pure incarnation of the ruthless American woman—selfish, demanding, destructive. Although she rarely played a mother, she was, on screen, a representation of exactly what Philip Wylie was talking about in his famous essay on Mom.

She was born Ruby Stevens in Brooklyn on July 16, 1907. Orphaned when she was four, she was raised in a series of foster homes. At thirteen she became a professional dancer, a trade she had mostly taught herself. Cast in a show called *The Noose,* she got her first break when, in the out-of-town tryouts, the show was rewritten and a chorine was needed as heroine. Miss Stanwyck got the part. She went from that play to stardom in *Burlesque* and was brought to Hollywood by Frank Capra for *Ladies of Leisure.*

In all of these she was a hard case, and even in 1940, when she scored one of her rare comedy hits (in *The Lady Eve*), she played a professional card sharp. Probably her finest piece of work, expressing the quintessential Stanwyck, was in *Double Indemnity* (1944), Billy Wilder's savage study of chilling sex and emotionless murder. Hers was the attraction of complete, unnerving dominance—her screen lovers never believed that any woman could be so purely evil. Fascinated, they always discovered too late that she was.

The young Stanwyck, looking softer, sweeter than one remembers her.

167

KATHARINE HEPBURN
The lady as star

With Barrymore in A Bill of Divorcement, *her first major hit (1932).*

THERE IS A STORY THAT when Katharine Hepburn appeared in the dormitory dining room on the first night of her freshman year at Bryn Mawr, clad in a courage-bolstering bright-red dress, there was a dead silence, broken at last by the loud drawl of an upperclassman. "Ah," she cried, "conscious beauty." It is said that Miss Hepburn did not reappear in the dining room for seven months, that she seldom slept in her own room for the next two years, preferring the floor of a friend's room in another dormitory.

Much of the Hepburn screen presence is summed up by the Bryn Mawr anecdote. She is indeed a conscious beauty. Yet she seems shy about it, adopting a set of brittle, concealing mannerisms which are both pseudo-tough and sweetly skittish. She radiates intelligence and pride in her intelligence, which extends even to the business aspects of her career. (She was one of the few stars whom Louis B. Mayer could not best in contract negotiations.) On screen she is seemingly cold but easily awakened to love, fun, displays of anger, contempt and wicked humor. She is, in short, that genuine Hollywood rarity, a contradictory personality.

Going from Bryn Mawr to stock company acting, to an up-and-down Broadway career, she was labeled in 1937, after five Hollywood years (starting with *Bill of Divorcement*), as box-office poison by the nation's exhibitors. The American moviegoer of the early thirties was not yet ready for Katharine Hepburn. With the flinty determination of her New England heritage, she returned to Broadway and succeeded magnificently in *The Philadelphia Story*, playing the part of an eccentric heiress for which she was absolutely perfect. She returned to Hollywood in 1939 for the film version which established her forever in the public mind as the perfect aristocrat.

The series of films she made with her good friend, Spencer Tracy, films which always revolved around a class conflict, in which Mr. Tracy brought the lady down to his realistic level and made her like it, solidified her position. Her best films of recent years—*The African Queen* and *Summertime*—have been in a similar vein.

She remains, in a way, as self-conscious as she was on her first day at Bryn Mawr. She knows she is haughty, aloof, shy. She also knows that she needs only a man of strength and worldliness to tame her shyness and free her spirit from the cage of the self and from the inhibitions of society. The drama of a Hepburn film, generally speaking, is the drama of the change from Katharine to Kate, just as in *The Taming of the Shrew* the drama was in the transformation of Katharina into Bonny Kate. Miss Hepburn, with her customary graceful intelligence, seems to know this. "I was fortunate to be born with a set of characteristics that were in public vogue," she says, acknowledging that the public of the late thirties was eager to see an aristocrat who would desert her inbred values for democratic fun. She was, on screen as in life, a good sport despite her heritage.

"I'm a personality as well as an actress. Show me an actress who isn't a personality, and you'll show me a woman who isn't a star." Here is the personality with her long-time friend and frequent costar, Spencer Tracy, and in The African Queen, *her best role.*

THE ATHLETES

Movies about team sports have generally proved to be financial failures. This is something of an oddity, given the American obsession for attending children's games. But in the late thirties and early forties, films starring athletes became consistent box-office successes. These, however, were all about individual performers in sports that required extreme grace of execution. Their appeal was double-edged.

The camera brought the spectator closer to the performer than he ever could have got in the stadium, allowing him to study . . . er . . . form. Even more interesting was the spectacle of the celebrity from a different medium succeeding in a new one.

That these athletic stars were not actors, or even particularly engaging personalities, did not seem to matter. You could hardly understand Sonja Henie, whose accent was as thick as her ankles. Johnny Weissmuller's dialogue consisted solely of gutturals and a handful of the simpler nouns, pronouns and verbs, so he got by as an actor, although Elmo Lincoln, the first screen Tarzan, was heard to mutter that the ape-man seemed "sissified." As for Miss Esther Williams, her athletic record was not as distinguished as the others, but she was prettier and she could speak English—sort of.

Sonja Henie won more Olympic skating titles than anyone in history, but she never won any acting awards. Her thespic style was as stolid as her skating style was graceful.

"Glub. Me Tarzan. Glub, glub. You Esther Williams."
She appears in Pagan Love Song. *Johnny Weismuller,*
converted Tarzan from a swinger of vines
into a water creature, reversing normal evolution.

The greatest athlete
ERROL FLYNN

In his autobiography Errol Flynn remarks, "As I went from one picture to another, the stereotyped roles I played stamped out of me my ambition to do finer things or to expect to be able to do them in Hollywood. When you're young, a beginner, you have a contract to fulfill, you have little to say about your roles. . . . You're hooked. With time I would lose my inner guts, my belief in myself even as an actor."

Flynn was, on the evidence of his own writing, a sincere man lacking the inner conviction to remain serious for very long. His answer to the problem of being forever cast in the public's mind as Captain Blood or Robin Hood was to squabble incessantly with his studio, his women, the roistering collection of he-men with whom he surrounded himself. "I do not know," he wrote, "to what extent this stereotyping of me—this handing me a sword and a horse . . . led to my rebellions, high jinks and horseplay over the globe, but I think it had plenty to do with it."

There are two phases to his career as an actor and two coincident phases in his career as a public personality. In phase number one he was a swashbuckler, a laughing cavalier, something like the later Douglas Fairbanks, although he lacked the fine edge Fairbanks put on his acrobatics and lacked, too, the finer dimensions of chivalry that were present in Fairbanks' films. Flynn, for all his peccadilloes, admitted that he did not really like women. Driven to them, he was also contemptuous of them. His technique with them, on screen and off, was to use the act of love as an act of aggression. Apparently his feminine audience sensed this, and in an era when they had responded mightily to Cagney's mastery of the grapefruit, they responded also to the Flynn style of degradation—which was to laugh at them even as they pursued him.

Flynn himself declared that "mostly I walked through my pictures." The Flynn walk, however, was equivalent to another man's run, and his screen character implied the rich-

Errol Flynn swashes, and Eugene Pallette is about to buckle. The movie is The Adventures of Robin Hood.

Rocky Mountain, *obviously one of the star's more painful roles.*

ness of Flynn's remarkably adventurous youth. He was born in Tasmania, where his highly conservative father had built a distinguished reputation as a marine biologist. Young Errol developed an early, strong, and lasting contempt for the staid and conservative life of his parents, and most of his life may be read as a rebellion against it. Running away from school in Australia, Flynn indulged in a life of petty crime and petty jobs until he set off for New Guinea, where he was briefly an extremely junior colonial officer, a fairly successful plantation manager, captain of a coastal sailing ship, a hunter for the forbidden bird of paradise, a gold miner and, finally a man who stood trial for murder, having killed a native participating in a raid on one of his jungle camps. Eventually he settled down to start a tobacco plantation, but he was no sooner embarked on that career than a small-time movie maker whom he had met in his wanderings telegraphed him an offer to appear in a film called *In the Wake of the Bounty*. Nothing came of the job immediately, but Flynn, smuggling a few diamonds to help out with his expenses, wandered by the most circuitous possible route to England where, eventually, he found work as an actor with the Northampton Repertory Company. The company, along with many others, went to Stratford one summer to appear in the drama festival and two of its productions were selected for showing in the West End. There Flynn was spotted by a Warner's scout. His first Hollywood part was as a corpse in *The Case of the Curious Bride*. Shortly thereafter, the studio took a chance on two unknowns, Flynn and Olivia de Havilland, as the romantic leads in *Captain Blood*. The picture and the two young players were wildly successful.

By 1937, Flynn had, with *The Adventures of Robin Hood*, consolidated his position as the screen's leading costume romantic.

Success, however, did not change the basic rebelliousness of his nature. He believed, with considerable justification, that he was underpaid, he disliked his parts, his marriage to Lili Damita was little more than a lengthy squabble. He poured a good deal more energy into his off-screen peccadilloes than he did into his work. Thus was born the great Flynn legend, which reached its height at the time of his trial on charges of statutory rape. His popularity waning, his money slipping through his fingers at an enormous rate, Flynn attempted to produce his own films but, in the process, suffered a mild heart attack and discovered that he now lacked the nerve to perform the feats of derring-do on which he had built his career.

He slipped into a drifting, aimless retirement, a used-up, washed-up profile. Then, suddenly, in the late fifties, he emerged as a character actor of considerable skill. As he had played his youthful self in the early days, he now began to play his mature self—a faded, somewhat alcoholic, faintly comic, and very weary old roué. The old gallantry was still present, but it was edged with the oddly dignified pathos of the man who is suddenly, shockingly aware of his mortality. He did fine work in *The Roots of Heaven, The Sun Also Rises* and as John Barrymore in *Too Much, Too Soon*. He died of a heart attack in 1960, not long after composing his own epitaph: "I want to be taken seriously. . . . I allow myself to be understood abroad as a colorful fragment in a drab world."

The many moods of Flynn. Above, he is at his most suavely elegant. Left, his exertions have told on him. Below, he at last has a good role—in The Sun Also Rises. Mel Ferrer is seen helping him to his feet after an unfortunate encounter with a bull at Pamplona.

JOHN GARFIELD *Depression's child*

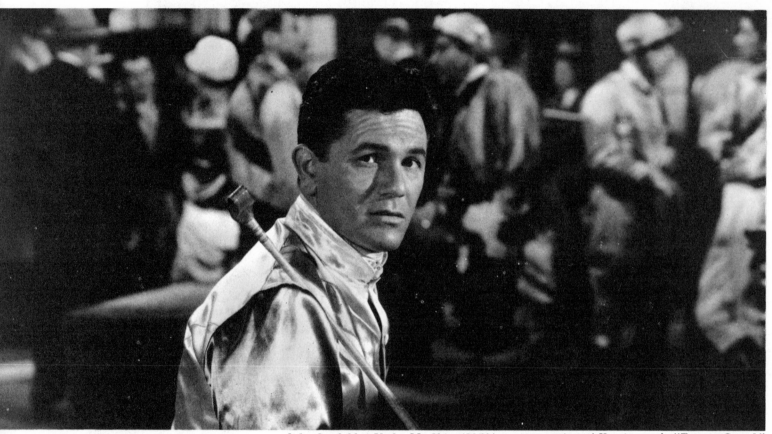

John Garfield in Under My Skin *(1950), screen version of Hemingway's "Twenty Grand."*

"IF HE WASN'T WINNING, he didn't know who he was." Thus the character of John Garfield as seen by a director who worked closely with him. Garfield was a tough, vital young man from the streets of New York, a graduate of the Neighborhood Playhouse and of the Group Theater to which he had brought a burning desire to learn the craft and the mystique of acting. Actually, Garfield was a natural—strong, sexy, motivated by a driving ambition that charged every part he ever played with his own restlessness and energy. Beneath the energy, but not obscured by it, one sensed a sweetness that made his ambition palatable. He was, to reverse the formula, a bad good man, wicked only in a boyish way.

A nice fellow hustling to improve himself, he was excellent in films like *Body and Soul,* in which he played a character much like himself. Temporarily bemused by the success ethic, the young fighter found himself groping in confusion for the values his better self sensed but could not practically

define. On screen Garfield reflected much of the urge for social mobility of a generation unsure as to whether the picket line or the night school would provide it.

Garfield himself was confused by the stardom thrust so suddenly upon him after he deserted the Group for the movies. That rather self-righteous collection of actors actually held a meeting to register their disapproval of Garfield's trip to Hollywood. Among his grievances was the Group's absurd failure to cast him as Golden Boy, relegating him to a minor part where he could watch the miscast Luther Adler do a part for which Garfield was born. The Group may have polished Garfield's talent, but its lingering effect on him was to create doubts about the value of his work, the reality of his talent. Its influence robbed him of the chance to enjoy the movie stardom which a part of his personality craved. He died of a heart attack in 1952. He was thirty-nine.

ORSON WELLES *The last typhoon*

Welles directed his wife, Rita Hayworth, in The Lady from Shanghai *(1948).*

KENNETH TYNAN ONCE REMARKED that Orson Welles was "a superb bravura director, a fair bravura actor, and a limited bravura writer; but an incomparable bravura personality." Which is a fair bravura summary of the man.

He came to the movies out of the theater, which he had come to after years of youthful wandering. The only prosaic thing about him was the place of his birth—Kenosha, Wisconsin. His mother was an aesthete, and his father was a sometime inventor who liked to hang around the lower levels of show business—with magicians, vaudevillians, ham actors of gaslight melodrama. His parents separated, and Welles spent his childhood first traveling with his mother, and after she died, drifting with his father. From her he acquired his taste for the finer things; from him he got

his passion for the cruder forms of theatricality.

His father died when Orson was fourteen; then, quitting school, he began to weave together the two disparate strands of his heritage. He traveled in the inconvenient ways a young man in search of himself adopts. He worked briefly at Dublin's Gate Theater, fought bulls in Spain, got his first American acting job with Katharine Cornell in *Romeo and Juliet,* then, in the depths of the depression, still in his early twenties, he went to work for the WPA's Federal Theater Project. There quickly followed the famous Mercury Theater and his celebrated radio adaptation of H. G. Wells's *War of the Worlds,* the furor over which quite overshadowed the valuable and exciting work he and his little troupe were doing in the barely living theater. Now a public figure, he

Welles in the title role of his directorial masterpiece, Citizen Kane.

A typically Wellesian angle on Citizen Kane. Ray Collins plays a departing political boss.

was plucked from the vine, exactly ripe, by Hollywood.

Welles was ready for Hollywood, but Hollywood was not ready for Welles. Today, lesser men than he regularly cause more turmoil in the studios with their independent productions, without producing works of comparable stature. But Hollywood then was completely dominated by the studio system and was unused to dealing with a man of the Gargantuan talents and appetites of Welles. He brought *Citizen Kane* in on time and at reasonable cost. He did the same with *The Magnificent Ambersons*. He was not, except in manner and talent, a profligate like Von Stroheim, and he made films that reputable critics believed to be utterly unique. It was a measure of Hollywood's lack of imagination that they still seem avant-garde when viewed today, though more than twenty years have intervened. He made other films after these masterpieces, and not one of them failed to be interesting. Some critics said his films were too self-conscious. In a way that is true. He insisted on calling attention to the fact that they were, indeed, movies, that is to say, art objects. This ran counter to common film practice, which is to be artless in its realism. Only now is the European avant-garde beginning to follow the Wellesian aesthetic.

Eventually, he left America for good, plagued by tax troubles, more deeply plagued by mediocrities who insisted on judging him either by a balance sheet or by standards of art too ordinary for applicability to his bursting talent. He said recently, "The cinema has no boundary; it is a ribbon of dream." More than any American since Griffith, he stretched that ribbon—almost to the breaking point.

Welles is a star, not because of any single part he played, but because he was a total movie maker who stamped his personality on entire films, because he insisted on using a medium of group creation as a means for a uniquely individual expression—which expression, we tend to forget (because of the artistic excitement they caused), was profoundly related to the new political and social values of New Deal America. Many film makers have made interesting social comments; a few have made great personal statements. Only Welles has combined both in our time.

Later Welles. Left, as Harry Lime in Sir Carol Reed's fine thriller, The Third Man. *Above, as he appeared in* Touch of Evil, *the last movie he directed for Hollywood. It was a wonderful study of bottom-of-the-barrel corruption.*

181

FIVE

PART FIVE

HEROES

It is a regrettable fact of life in that we in America have produced few heroes. One searches in vain for a man who has attained true heroic stature since 1945. One reason for this seems fairly obvious: the complexity of our institutions tends to limit the role of the individual—he may contribute, but it is impossible for him to dominate.

Robert W. White, the psychologist, has suggested that the inability of the individual "to make things happen" is one of the sources of neurosis in modern society. This being true, it is not surprising to find that no truly heroic new personalities have appeared on the screen in the postwar years, and that we have clung, through those years, to a handful of aging superstars who established their screen characters in the thirties.

There are, of course, purely technical reasons for the longevity of these stars. With the decline of the studio system in Hollywood it became increasingly difficult to build a youthful personality by carefully placing him in roles which would reinforce a predetermined image. For the most part, the screen actor today free-lances from studio to studio, taking whatever roles are remunerative and within his range. In addition, the B picture, traditional training ground for young stars, has virtually disappeared, and there is no inexpensive way to determine which roles a young man may play best and which aspects of his character can be used as the basis for the creation of a strong screen personality.

Then, too, the old idea that whatever acting a star does should take place within the boundaries of a strong, previously well-defined personality is now held in considerable contempt. Finally, it is almost impossible, in our cynical times, to undertake the kind of publicity build-up that would give an embryo star a suitably romantic and larger-than-life off-screen prsonality. Everyone today wants to know what he is "really" like, and so the would-be star submits to public psychoanalysis, even seems to enjoy the process. To adapt an old saw, "No man is a hero to his analyst."

The five stars dealt with in the following sections created strong and appealing public personalities during the thirties. They had the opportunity to play, over and over again, roles similar to one another, thereby creating strong images of themselves—images which lingered in the minds of a large pool of fans who, despite television and other distractions, were willing to seek out these now aging creations in new films. They achieved, as a result, their greatest financial successes in the forties and fifties. Careful professionals who knew how to guard their images, they remained enigmatic, preferring to allow the audience to gather, from the hints they carefully supplied, its own ideas about who and what they were. In so doing they tapped the collective American unconscious and became repositories and symbols of our longing for heroism in its various forms and settings.

The thirties may well pass into our history as the last age in which it still seemed possible for the individual to become, through his own efforts, a moral and physical hero. The fact that in the forties and fifties all of these stars—Cooper, Bogart, Gable, Tracy, Stewart—became the objects of almost cultish, surely nostalgic, hero worship indicates our knowledge that something is missing from our age.

GARY COOPER

GARY COOPER WAS, by common consent, the archetypal American. Just before he died he said: "Everybody asks me how come you're around so long. Well, I always attribute it to playing the part of Mr. Average Joe American. Just an average guy from the middle of the U.S.A. And then, I guess I got to believe it . . . Gary Cooper, an Average Charlie who became a movie actor."

Cooper, as he undoubtedly knew, was oversimplifying in this summation. For instance, there was the matter of his appearance. He was, by any standard, a handsome man. Yet, by his manner, Cooper depreciated the fact. This was not because of any false modesty. It was rather an insistence on the subordination of superficials to matters of deeper import. He seemed to sense that it was essential for his audience to be comfortable in his presence. He preferred, for reasons of both art and personal taste, understatement. His way was to imply strength rather than to insist upon it.

His first important assignment was in *The Winning of Barbara Worth* (1926), and his big scene was with Ronald Colman, the actor Cooper most admired. He was to die in Colman's arms, and he received this bit of advice from the Englishman: "Easy does it, old boy. Good scenes make good actors. Actors don't make a scene. My own feeling is that all you have to do is take a nap, and every woman who sees the picture is going to cry her eyes out."

Cooper napped—and scored his first major success. Through the years he developed this technique of non-acting to its highest point. One of his last directors, Anthony Mann, said, "Something in those eyes tells you fantastic things. I've directed many stars, but never have I seen such eyes. They are at once electric, honest, devastating. And he knows how to look through them. . . . No one can so graphically reveal his thoughts by the look on his face."

The thoughts of Cooper's screen character turned often to the question of morality. He believed in the standard American variety, and he took it seriously, as a code to live by. The drama of a Cooper film arose from the conflict between a man who based his conduct on the commonly accepted code and those who claimed they did, but actually proceeded on a business-as-usual basis. From this stemmed the immutability of Cooper's appeal. He behaved as we would have

One of Cooper's first successes, Lilac Time, (1928) with Colleen Moore.

Gary Cooper in his Academy Award–winning performance in Sergeant York (1941).

One American folk hero plays another. Cooper as Lou Gehrig, in Pride of the Yankees. *Below, he Americanizes a different sort of hero, Venetian traveler Marco Polo. Ernest Truex plays the man who doesn't like firecrackers.*

Cooper as a Hemingway hero, Frederick Henry, in A Farewell to Arms. *Critics found much in common between Hemingway's literary vision and Cooper's screen character. Adolphe Menjou is Coop's sophisticated companion. The legs do not belong to costar Helen Hayes.*

liked to behave were not the world too much with us.

But there was more to the matter than this. The thing that really riled Cooper was invasion of privacy. The suspense in a classic Cooper film was generated by seeing how much abuse he would take before, at long last, and with great weariness, he would unwind his lanky frame and go after his tormentors. It was his habit to exhaust all manner of rational appeal, even exhibit a willingness to submit to unmanning abuse, before strapping on his guns. Abstract principle was all right, and he would defend it, but more often he rose to defend himself and his conception of himself.

High Noon was a perfect example of this. He stayed to fight the bandit gang not for the sake of the town, which had long since proved itself unworthy of the effort, not for any social abstraction, but because the gang posed a supreme threat not only to his health but to his personal morality. He fought to defend his right to self-determination, his right to be himself as he wanted to be.

Cooper's screen personality was the honest product of a man noted for giving fair measure in his dealings both as a professional and as an individual. The career was a masterpiece of understatement and of timing, for Cooper managed it himself, shrewdly altering the externals of setting, costume, even film genre, but always making sure he touched home base every two or three pictures. A native of the West, personally a devotee of its outdoor amusements, he made certain that the intervals between Westerns were never long. He knew as well as any one that his roots were there. "It's always been a question," he told writer Thomas Morgan, "whether to let the public see what they expect or whether you should give them something new. It always comes up. There are things Gary Cooper shouldn't do, things that offer great opportunities actingwise . . ."

He was rather better in comedy than one expected; he was superb as a Hemingway hero (a man, as Leslie Fiedler pointed out, with virtually the same values as the screen Westerner). In short, he extended his range more than he would have had to, and perhaps this was one of the reasons

for his undiminishing popularity. More than other actors of similar limitations, he offered as many variations on his basic theme as possible. He guarded his screen self jealously, and he once declared: "An oil man is allowed to deplete 27 per cent annually as the oil is used up. An industrialist can depreciate his equipment as it ages. Now all I have to sell is me—this body of mine. If it's maimed or broken I can't work. And it ages just as certainly as machine tools. But do they let me depreciate it? Heck, no."

The thought is not as important as the image—that of an entrepreneur handling a difficult enterprise with all the canniness at his command. He did that with a curious, engaging lack of ego. He was here, as in his screen roles, the easy, confident professional, so good at what he did that the doing was the only self-assertion he needed to make. The rewards were inherent in the means, although of course the ends were pleasant enough—and Cooper seemed to revel in being the well-tailored, quietly cultured international celebrity at home in salons both social and artistic.

He was not, of course, a simple cowhand. His family was well-to-do, his father a justice of the Montana Supreme Court and a gentleman rancher. Cooper learned the ways of the Westerner as a boy, but he also spent three years in an English public school. He went to college for three years and thought of becoming a commercial artist. Visiting his family in Los Angeles (where his father was working on a case), he ran into old ranch friends who were working as stunt riders in silent Westerns. He joined them and, through a combination of circumstance and intelligent self-interest, won his role in *Barbara Worth*.

A starring role in a medium-budget Western, a memorable bit in *Wings* as a doomed flier, and co-starring roles with Clara Bow and Lupe Velez brought him to the sound barrier as a rising star. His first sound film, *The Virginian*, was, as he said, "the big one—you had to survive the transition to talking pictures. *The Virginian* put me over the hump and made millions." It also was a film with a great deal of "yup" and "nope" dialogue. In his late years Cooper banned both words from his scripts. There was no point in giving grist to the joke mills. Like his heroes, he took no foolish chances—only calculated risks.

The film, of course, is Fred Zinnemann's
High Noon. *For his portrayal*
Cooper won his second Academy Award.

HUMPHREY BOGART

"Speculative, sardonic, sourly lisping" Humphrey Bogart lived in a gray area where you could arrest him if you cared to apply the law's letter or sympathize with him if you were broad-minded. The legality of the character he played was less important than the central fact of his existence—which was loneliness. The Westerner was lonely, too, but that was a matter of choice; he valued solitude, even needed its restorative quality. Bogart's loneliness was edged by desperation and was accompanied by that special kind of unshaven squalor that is the mark of bachelorhood in a modern American city—unscraped dishes in the sink, rye whisky in the file drawer of the desk, a scrambled newspaper tented crazily on the floor next to the ugly, worn, comfortable easy chair commanding views of the television set and the bedroom of the pretty girl who lives across the airshaft and draws the shades carelessly when she undresses.

His special knowledge was of the jungle of the city at night—which clubs the syndicate ran, which one-arm restaurants served good coffee, which hotels a whore could use, which streets were safe to walk upon after midnight. It was this detailed knowledge that set Bogart apart from the ordinary lonely male; it was the rightness of setting, mood and dialogue that established our empathy with him. It was the toughness—and the supreme self-reliance—with which he met loneliness that established this unlikely character as a screen favorite.

Bogart, in his early incarnation as a gangster, lacked the dimension of tragedy which Warshow found in the work of Cagney and Robinson. He was neither charming nor especially megalomaniacal. Lacking the cheerful, All-American bounce of Cagney's psychotic, he was much more the brooding outsider. He also lacked Robinson's drive for power, and you could not blame society for his malformed character. His was a purely personal, purely psychological defect.

He switched to the side of the law, more or less, in John

The role that made Bogart famous, Duke Mantee in The Petrified Forest.

Huston's brilliant *The Maltese Falcon* in 1940. In the first—and still the greatest—private-eye film, he was, as Tynan says, "still the same wry brute, but more insidiously immoral since now there was a righteous justification for his savagery." World War II killed the gangster film, and with one or two notable exceptions the genre has stayed dead. Public interest in domestic criminals was, of course, quite blotted out by the scope of the crimes committed in the course of war, and the war itself offered movie makers an unparalleled backdrop for adventure. The gangster drama suddenly seemed very small potatoes indeed. The decline of murderous gangs in the postwar years (the nation's criminals, according to mythology, having become more subtle and businesslike in their operations) made the old-style crime films seem rather quaint.

Bogart's basic character was more adaptable than that of other members of the screen underworld, it being the product of inner, rather than societal, forces. In the war years his weary, saturnine presence, informed by his terrible awareness of both his own and the world's weaknesses, was

enlisted in the cause of the Allies. His devotion to that cause was frequently ambiguous, as in *Casablanca*. Like Cooper's Man of the West, Bogart could get interested in a fight for justice or principle only when his own, direct stake in the outcome was made painfully clear to him. He reacted with surly suspicion when someone appealed to his better nature. "Nobody gets the best of Fred C. Dobbs," he snarled in the postwar *Treasure of the Sierra Madre*, and the remark was *echt* Bogart. His loneliness was based on suspicion of everyone's motives, and the statement of this basic fact was the everlasting theme of his life's work. It accounted for his defensive inwardness, his unbreakable façade.

His screen personality formed an interesting contrast with Cooper's Westerner, as well as with the sunny city man first projected by Fairbanks. Cooper's silences were open, even friendly and respectful. Bogart's were glowering, neurotically inspired. He was painful evidence of what the city can do to a man, how it can brutalize and wound his sensibility, rob him of all emotion except a cheap sentimentality. And, because he was usually found scraping along in some mar-

"Nobody gets the best of Fred C. Dobbs." Bogart in another fine Huston film, The Treasure of the Sierra Madre *(1947).*

Bogart in Beat the Devil, *the John Huston–Truman Capote satire on adventure movies, which Bogart himself did not appreciate but which found a small but fanatically loyal audience. Jennifer Jones appears at the left.*

Bogie and Baby in The Big Sleep, *one of action director Howard Hawks's best films. In it Bogart had one of his perfect roles, as Raymond Chandler's private eye, Philip Marlowe.*

No one fitted a trench coat better than Bogart. Here he appears in The Barefoot Contessa.

ginal business enterprise, as proprietor of a night club or a detective agency, he was a bitter parody of the up-and-at-'em values of the Fairbanks character. Bogart, one sensed, had found that technique terribly wanting, an experience which, along with a string of love affairs gone sour, accounted for the resemblance of his face to a closed fist.

As for Bogart himself, he had little experience of more expansive vistas than the city afforded. He was the son of a well-to-do New York doctor and a successful commercial artist named Maude Humphrey. One of her works, of Bogie as a beautiful baby, had adorned the packages of a well-known brand of baby food. After restless and cursory schooling, Bogart joined the Navy in World War I, acquiring, when his ship was shelled, the partly paralyzed upper lip that accounted for his deadly lisp and the tight set of his mouth.

He is credited with uttering, for the first time anywhere, the immemorial cry of the stage juvenile, "Tennis, anyone?" in one of his youthful Broadway appearances in the twenties. He had no notable success in his first try at the movies and had to return to Broadway and the part of Duke Mantee in *The Petrified Forest* before Hollywood paid any attention to him. Even then, Leslie Howard had to threaten to withdraw from the film version if Warner's refused to cast him.

From that point on, the tensely knotted Bogart personality was never absent from the screen. Close observers saw the new dimension Bogart brought to the tough-guy part. Said Jerry Wald: "Bogart was liked by audiences because he had, in the toughest gangster roles, a pathetic quality . . . He always gained sympathy." Said Stanley Kramer: "He had the damnedest façade of any man I ever met in my life. He was playing Bogart all the time, but he was really a big, sloppy bowl of mush."

Lauren Bacall, his wife, thought he was "truly a gentle soul . . . this was a rather old-fashioned fellow. He really believed in the original concept of the home and a wife's place in the home." Nunnally Johnson said, "He never stopped thinking how he could stir things up . . . He was an ingrained mischief maker." In short, all the things that contributed to his screen character were part of the natural Bogart—the odd belief in chivalry, so frequently disappointed that it was masked by cynicism, the almost sadistic streak of gallows humor, the sentiment that motivated the decent acts of his screen character. Bogart himself declared that his method was "to give the impression I'm not acting. . . . You think it. If you think it, you'll look it. If you feel sorry, you'll look sorry."

The result was summed up by a man who knew best what

Bogart's Academy Award winning performance in the brilliant adventure-comedy-romance, The African Queen *(1951).*

Bogart was trying to do. Raymond Chandler, creator of one of Bogart's best roles (Philip Marlowe in *The Big Sleep*), declared: "Bogart can be tough without a gun. Also, he has a sense of humor that contains that grating undertone of contempt. Ladd is hard, bitter and occasionally charming, but he is after all a small boy's idea of a tough guy. Bogart is the genuine article. Like Edward G. Robinson, all he has to do to dominate a scene is to enter it."

CLARK GABLE

WHEN CLARK GABLE DIED, the New York *Times* editorialized: "Gable was as certain as the sunrise. He was consistently and stubbornly all Man." There was nothing enigmatic about him. He was, for two generations, the popular ideal of the American male, open, uncomplicated, tough yet gentle, an appreciator of the simple American pleasures—rare steak, raw whisky, racy women.

Gable was a rare screen star in that he appealed strongly and equally to both sexes. Men saw in him a good companion for a carouse, a fight, an all-night poker session. Women saw in his lopsided grin the eternal small boy who, according to mythology, resides in all men. He might be rough at times, but they knew he could be gentled and if, from time to time, they were wise enough to let him roam free they could be sure he would return, probably looking a little sheepish. His appeal was all on the surface. He did not hide his strength under a lazy exterior like Cooper and, unlike him, there was no moral fervor lurking beneath the surface. Quite the opposite: he was rather devilishly amoral. He made no statement beyond that which was immediately apprehended upon his first entrance in a film.

But for all his simple masculine appeal, there was one intriguing feature about the parts Gable played. He performed a sexual function that neither Bogart nor Cooper usually attempted. Bogart's relationship with women was hostile, Cooper's remotely chivalrous, and neither was anything but superficial, almost casual, with women. They had more important things in mind. But Gable's screen character was built upon his ability to cut across class lines to accomplish the sexual awakening of frigid, upper-class women.

His first important role, in *A Free Soul* (1930), cast him as a gangster who humbled proud Norma Shearer with, among other things, a sharp right to the jaw. He accomplished much the same thing in *Red Dust* (1932) for Mary Astor, though he gave her up for tough, good-guyish Jean Harlow. Some twenty years later, in a remake of *Red Dust* called *Mogambo*, he proved the agelessness of his appeal, by knocking the same kind of sexual sense into proud, chilly

Gable and wife, Carole Lombard.

The King. The film, of course, is Gone With the Wind.

Gable with Joan Crawford in The Dancing Lady.

Grace Kelly. And, of course, he contributed the definitive portrait of the irresistible nature of low lustiness as Rhett Butler in *Gone with the Wind*.

Interestingly, in his own marriages he was torn between the chilly sophisticates and the down-to-earth types. Life being unlike a screen play, he found happiness only with the latter type—Carole Lombard and Kay Williams.

It is easy enough to understand why Gable was elected "King" of Hollywood in a poll of editors conducted by Ed Sullivan in 1938. Though his films carried far less social commentary than those of Cooper and Bogart, he was very much an expression of a nation's feelings during the Depression Decade. Gable elicited an immediate and direct response from his audiences, though he played almost exclusively in highly irrelevant films—lightweight comedies and adventures, both historical and contemporary, that had little to do with the great questions of the day.

He was a roguish, down-to-earth, adventurous man, and

a major part of his appeal was his lack of roots. Gable was at home everywhere—in oil fields, in city streets and penthouses, astride a horse, in sundry jungles, in any historical era. Everywhere he was the democratic man, both in his contempt for the alleged thinness of aristocratic blood and in his envious attraction to the good, soft life of the upper classes. He nearly always played a self-made man and the role carried with it a built-in contempt for the man who inherited his wealth or was not driven by the same lust for life that motivated him.

As for women, it was always a toss-up whether, having forced a high-born heroine to admit the earthy urgency of her desires, he would be satisfied or, having accomplished this task, would abandon her for the common woman who understood all this in her bones and could please him without need of his night-school courses in the art of love.

How appealing all this was! The men, of course, saw in Gable a man capable of living a life of adventure and easy

With Norma Shearer in Strange Interlude *(1932). He had become a star opposite her in* A Free Soul *the year before.*

One of the Oscar-winning moments of It Happened One Night *(1934). Gable, Colbert, film, all won Awards.*

Postwar Gable. With Keenan Wynn in The Hucksters.

conquest just like the one they themselves conducted in their fantasies. The women could lead multiple fantasy lives in his pictures. They could imagine themselves as the aristocratic ladies first fighting off, then yielding to, his rough advances. But, once the picture ended, they could console themselves with the knowledge that he was also attracted to ordinary women.

As for Gable himself, his early life was as restless as that of one of his screen characters. His father was a roving oil field boomer who for the most part left his son to his own devices. His mother died not long after giving him birth. Periods of prosperity and tranquillity alternated with periods of troubled restlessness. A stepmother gentled him and gave him what maternal love he experienced.

When he was fifteen he left his Ohio farm home to work in Akron. There he worked backstage with a stock company (salary zero) during his free time. He left to join his father in the oil fields after his stepmother died, then left that miserable existence for another city and another theatrical troupe. It ran out of funds in Butte, Montana, and he drifted to the lumber camps and then to Portland, where he met Josephine Dillon, director of a local stock company. Eventually they married, briefly and unhappily. Together they went to Holly-wood, where she worked as a drama coach and he got some movie bits. Stock assignments in Los Angeles and Houston, work in New York, then the lead in the Los Angeles production of *The Last Mile*—the part which had made Spencer Tracy a star in New York—led him back to the movies.

Now a more polished performer, he had the usual troubles securing work ("His ears are too big," cried Jack Warner upon seeing a test) but did well enough for M-G-M to take a chance on him opposite Shearer in *A Free Soul;* the theory was that he would be too innocuous either to upset or to upstage Irving Thalberg's wife. Things did not quite work out that way. Four years later Gable was in the box-office top ten, was earning $3,500 a week and had won an Academy Award for *It Happened One Night.* "You know," he said shortly before he died, "this King stuff is pure bullshit. I eat and sleep and go to the bathroom just like everyone else. There's no special light that shines inside me and makes me a star. I'm just a lucky slob from Ohio. I happened to be in the right place at the right time and I had a lot of smart guys helping me—that's all." There is more truth than modesty to his statement. But he did have, on screen, the special arrogance of a man who was comfortably sure of his identity and of his untrammeled masculinity.

Neither door nor woman could withstand the aroused Gable.

Tracy plays the flinty judge in Judgment at Nuremberg, *for which he received his seventh Oscar nomination.*

First of his successive Academy Award roles, Captains Courageous.

SPENCER TRACY

AMONG HIS FELLOW PLAYERS, Spencer Tracy is regarded as the finest screen actor of them all. Gable was on record as thinking him the best, and Bogart agreed. "You don't see the mechanism working, the wheels turning. He covers up. He never overacts or is hammy. He makes you believe he is what he is playing." Richard Widmark has said that "in my adult years, the man I have admired most in acting is Spencer Tracy. What an actor should be is exemplified, for me, by him. I like the reality of his acting. It's honest and seems so effortless, even though what Tracy does is the result of damn hard work and concentration. . . . He doesn't talk much about acting, but he knows it all."

Tracy himself is gruff, grumpy and, on occasion, highly temperamental. He growls: "Aw, why don't they leave me alone? I am old and fat, and I've got a face like a beat-up barn door." Since the beginning of his film career he has had the habit of dropping out of sight for days at a time,

Boom Town. *Gable thought Tracy the screen's best actor.*

sometimes out of rebelliousness at a bad part, sometimes just to brood. Preparing a role, he trains like a prize fighter. Says one of his friends: "He diets, locks himself in his room and won't see anybody. He studies his script until he knows it by heart. You'd think every picture was his first—he gets so nervous and edgy and unsure of himself."

Born in Milwaukee, he served in the Navy in World War I, returned to finish high school, then went on to Ripon College, in Wisconsin. One of his teachers there told writer Bill Davidson that "Tracy seemed to find escape from his own restlessness in the problems of the characters he was playing. He was best at portraying tough, brutal men—which he wasn't."

After little more than a year of college he went to New York to study at the American Academy of Dramatic Art. He roomed with Pat O'Brien, made his stage debut in *R.U.R.* in 1922. He married in 1923, and with the tragedy of his son's total deafness at birth driving him, he began to emerge as a reliable stage actor. His portrayal of Killer Mears in *The Last Mile* led to a Hollywood contract in 1930. Cast almost permanently as a tough guy, he himself gained a reputation as a hard man to handle. Not until he signed with M-G-M and played a priest in *San Francisco* (with Gable and Jeanette MacDonald), then the almost-victim of a lynch mob in *Fury*, did he begin to emerge as an actor of considerable

203

range. He won Academy Awards in 1937 for *Captains Courageous* and in 1938 for *Boys Town.* In 1941 he was teamed for the first time with Katharine Hepburn, with whom he has since made seven films and who, according to friends, has broadened him intellectually as well as emotionally.

Miss Hepburn has said she is "a personality as well as an actress. Show me an actress who isn't a personality and you'll show me a woman who isn't a star. A star's personality has to shine through." It is a sound generalization, but more difficult to apply to her friend Tracy than to any other contemporary actor. It is impossible to characterize Spencer Tracy through a discussion of the kind of role he plays (there are too many of them in too many genres). Of late, he has tended toward foxy grandpa parts in which he implies much knowledge while saying little. But in the past lie straightforward leading-man roles, a quite excellent *Dr. Jekyll and Mr. Hyde,* extremely funny, sexy comic parts, a succession of priests, roughnecks, bemused suburban husbands and criminals. To all of these roles he has brought some uniquely personal appeal, one which has made him an indestructible star. But what is it? You cannot describe his gruff, bluff, reasonable, humorous screen presence and let it go at that. There is something more to Tracy.

It can be seen clearly in *Bad Day at Black Rock,* his best picture of recent years. In it he plays a gentle, inexplicably sad city man who, on a sentimental errand, encounters astonishing hostility in a small, desolate desert town. He slides affably along, turning the other cheek, until at long last the town's leading bully, played by Ernest Borgnine, insists on drawing him into a fight. Tracy, for purposes of the script, has only one usable arm, but in a burst of action lasting little more than a minute on the screen, he utterly destroys Borgnine. In the process, he hardly moves; there is only the vicious chop of his arm, delivering karate blows with deadly, angry precision while Tracy's impassive face registers nothing —except, perhaps, a tiny flicker of contempt.

Here is the essential Tracy, in effortless control of himself and the situation, implying the deepest kind of emotion, but insisting on nothing. All his energy is focused on the task at hand; there are no irrelevant emotions. As an actor he never generalizes, he concentrates fiercely on his specific, immediate objective. The result is the subtle revelation of inner tension. It is in conflict with his surface control, and out of this conflict he generates the energy of his typical performance, the energy which draws the attention of the audience irresistibly to him.

Father of the Bride, *morning, afternoon and evening.*

JAMES STEWART

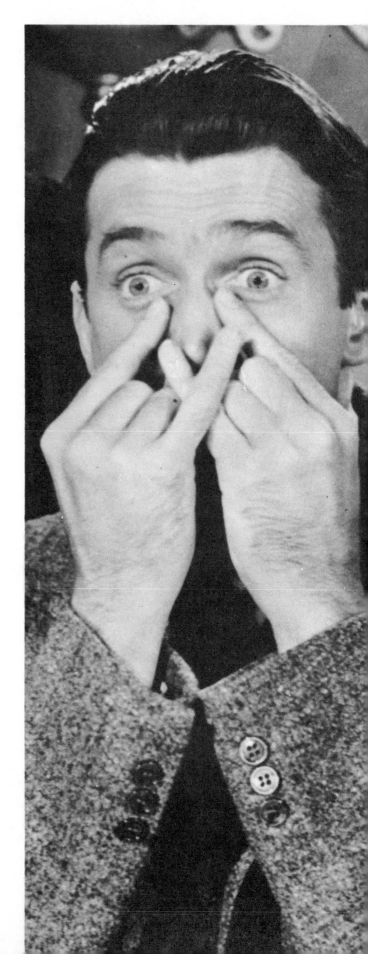

JAMES STEWART HAS GROWN UP under the eyes of the entire
nation, but like the favorite son whose maturity is never quite
believed in, he remains "Jimmy," and in the mind's eye, he
is forever the gawky, awkward, slow-speaking, whiny-voiced
youth of his prewar comedy successes. In truth, however,
Mr. James Stewart, now fifty-four, a general in the Air Force
Reserve, a sure-footed businessman who was among the first
Hollywood stars to work out a percentage-of-the-profits ar-
rangement on his movies, has not made an awkward move in
years. And, although the power he can generate as an actor
is not generally commented upon domestically, he won the
Venice Film Festival award for best actor for his work in
Anatomy of a Murder (1959). Like most of his work since
1945, his performance as a small-town lawyer was raw, edgy
and full of nervous energy.

Indeed, it was the nervousness that first set Stewart apart
from other stars who came to prominence in the thirties playing *vox populi* roles. Most of them—Cooper, Fonda, Randolph
Scott, John Wayne—played with commanding quietness. It
took a great deal to stir them, and some of them still had sleep
in their eyes even as they finally rose to their climactic action.
Stewart was never like that. He was certainly shy, but he was
also eager, to the point of falling all over himself. He wished
desperately to please the girl, to do the right thing. He was
easily diverted from his primary objectives and frequently
was hoodwinked, but in the end, and with a puppyish kind
of scramble, he would achieve his objectives.

Most of his early films were, in effect, studies in the learning process. By trial and error Stewart was initiated into the
ways of the world, and the climax was usually achieved when
Stewart, his integrity still intact, but his illusions dissipated,
attained his ambition without losing himself. In a sense, he
played a modern variant on that favorite American legend,
the Horatio Alger tale. Everything was pluck and luck with
him, and although he was a most appealing fellow, he was
not, as a rule, a prime mover of the plot. Things happened to
him, and though it was possible for him, in his inept way, to
convert good luck to bad (or vice versa), he was more a re-
actor than an originator. In his befuddlement over what was
happening to him, he symbolized the feelings of a good many
Americans in troubled times; in his good nature, and in his
clinging to the rural virtues which the very sound of his voice
summoned up, he was a reassuring link with the world of
Norman Rockwell paintings, large families, comfortable

Stewart as the barefoot boy with cheek . . .

homes, small-town pleasures and romanticized adolescence.

There was nothing accidental in this. Stewart's father was the inheritor and proprietor of the hardware store in Indiana, Pennsylvania, and Stewart learned from him frugality, piety, devotion to such ideals as patriotism and service, and, of course, the quiet sense of humor which has worn so well. His interests as a child were both athletic and artistic. At Mercersburg Academy he went out for football and track, but he also was art editor of the yearbook and active in the orchestra, glee club and dramatic group. He went on to Princeton, as his father had before him, and studied architecture. In the Triangle Club, the dramatic society, there was a fantastic flux of talent at the time. Joshua Logan, José Ferrer, Myron McCormick and Bretaigne Windust were all at Princeton, and Stewart worked with them. Billy O'Grady, M-G-M's chief talent scout, saw one of their performances, in which Stewart was one of a number of female impersonators, and remembered him as "the only one who didn't ham it up."

Logan roomed with Stewart on one of the club's tours and begged him to try acting as a career. Stewart insisted that he could not go against his father's wishes. Logan asked him if he couldn't at least try summer stock with him, with the now-famous University Players in Falmouth, Massachusetts. Stewart said he had promised to clerk in the hardware store back home. Logan finally said, "If you won't call your father and ask him, I will." At that Stewart got on the phone and persuaded his father to let him try. In addition to the Princeton contingent (minus Ferrer) the players included, in the summer of 1932, Henry Fonda, Margaret Sullavan and Kent Smith. There has probably never been a stock company with so many successful graduates.

That summer a play called *Goodbye Again* had a pre-Broadway tryout at Falmouth, and Stewart had two lines. As a chauffeur, he was called upon to enter, say, "Mrs. Mainwaring's car is waiting." After being told to wait, he drawled his reply, "Mrs. Mainwaring's going to be sore as hell." It wasn't much, but somehow Stewart managed to bring down the house with it. A visiting critic from New York wrote, "It seems apropos to say a few words about James Stewart, a player in this mad piece who is on stage for exactly three minutes. Yet before this gentleman exits he makes a definite impression on the audience because he makes them laugh so hard."

That fall, after a fling in a flop, Stewart was engaged for

. . . the film is Mr. Smith Goes to Washington.

Mr. Smith in a state of high, typically American dudgeon over the discovery that there are crooks in high places.

the same part on Broadway. He had six more roles in the next two years and in *Yellow Jack* was praised for a performance that was "simple, sensitive and true." *Yellow Jack,* according to one critic, "might have been a more impressive spectacle had the other characters taken their cue from Mr. Stewart."

Grady brought him to the Coast to play a reporter in *Murder Man,* Tracy's first picture under his new M-G-M contract. Stewart was not impressive, being too tall to play a character known as Shorty. In his own words, he "was all hands and feet and didn't know what to do with either." Nevertheless, he made more than twenty-five pictures in the next five years, including *You Can't Take It with You, Mr. Smith Goes to Washington, Destry Rides Again, No Time for Comedy* and *The Philadelphia Story,* for which he won the Academy Award that went on permanent display in his father's hardware store.

Then, at thirty-three, before America entered the war Stewart joined the Air Corps after a heroic eating bou designed to get his weight up over the minimum. He entered as a private but, because of his flying skill, rose to colonel leading one thousand plane strikes against Germany. H had, in direct contradiction to his screen character, a talen for command, and he won the Air Medal and the Distin guished Flying Cross with oak leaf clusters. When he re turned to Hollywood he had a clause inserted in his contrac which enjoined the studio from exploiting his war record.

He attempted to resume his old roles, but began to receive notices like "Jimmy Stewart is still exuding boyish charm in lethal doses." Undoubtedly Stewart himself was tired of the old stuff, especially after his wartime accomplishments. A any rate, he embarked on a vigorous campaign to change his image. In 1948 he played a hard-bitten police reporter in *Call Northside 777* and the headmaster involved with homo sexuals in Hitchcock's *Rope*. He returned to Broadway to replace Frank Fay in *Harvey*, then did the screen version before going into a string of salty, hard-bitten Westerns, notably *Winchester '73* and *Broken Arrow*, some Hitchcock suspense dramas and some fair screen biographies—*The Stratton Story, Carbine Williams, The Glenn Miller Story* and *The Spirit of St. Louis.*

Stewart still gangles and he still drawls—he can't really help that. But he is much tougher now, even grizzled-looking on occasion. The result is a very appealing screen character, much underrated by connoisseurs. The charm of the simple, small-town boy is there. One is always certain as to the nature of his character's background, the place where he learned his values. But the man himself is now a prime mover, capable of thinking things out for himself and of moving surely to set things right. In *Two Rode Together* (1961) he was, and very convincingly, a corrupt town marshal whose home was a bordello, a guide and Indian fighter who would take up a search for kidnaped children only after he had been handsomely paid in advance for his services by the poorest train of immigrants ever rounded up by central casting. He had come a long way from being the bumbling boy next door. A wonderful world of corruption is opening up for his screen characterizations; the irony of presenting his drawl and his gawkiness as the mannerisms of a tough, cynical and worldly older man is delicious. His best work may well lie ahead of him and that, somehow, is reassuring. There are precious few male stars of his generation left. He may well be, in fact, the last of the great men.

Mr. Stewart takes his ease on the set of Broken Arrow.

THE

PART SIX

FORTIES

In *Prater Violet*, Christopher Isherwood has one of his characters say: "The film studio of today is really the palace of the sixteenth century. There one sees what Shakespeare saw: the absolute power of the tyrant, the courtiers, the flatterers, the jesters, the cunningly ambitious intriguers. There are fantastically beautiful women, there are incompetent favorites. There are great men who are suddenly disgraced. There is the most insane extravagance, and unexpected parsimony over a few pence. There is enormous splendor, which is a sham; and also horrible squalor hidden behind the scenery. There are vast schemes, abandoned because of some caprice. There are secrets which everybody knows and no one speaks of. There are even two or three honest advisers. These are the court fools, who speak the deepest wisdom in puns, lest they should be taken seriously. They grimace, and tear their hair privately, and weep."

The studio described existed in England, but what is of interest to us is that the studio-as-palace reached its greatest flowering in Hollywood during the war years and, having achieved a megalomaniac's dream, almost immediately subsided. The dream palaces continue to exist, but they are inhabited by a race of Lears, surrounded by bright young men intent on picking up what profitable baubles they can, while the old dynasts dream of those wartime days when every week ninety million Americans went out to the movies. Hollywood is now a second-class power among industrial empires. What is fascinating is that its days of darkest depression and its days of greatest commercial glory occurred during the same decade—the forties—in the wink of an historical eye.

The films of the prosperous period were uniformly mediocre. During the war Hollywood turned out a standard product, technically expert, often lushly mounted, but vapid in the ways that count—story, direction, character. The social unrest of the thirties had produced a good deal of restiveness about the standard film formulas, a feeling that new times demanded a new seriousness in movies. But war and the need to produce escapist entertainment greatly heightened the trend toward the safe and sure. In addition, with competing amusements curtailed by shortages and rationing, the movies found that it was almost impossible to produce a film that failed at the box office—unless it were a rare try at a serious movie.

Then came 1947, which was, as Roland Barber put it, "a year of decision for the Industry—except that the industry didn't know it, made no decision, and thereby sanctioned its own decline. The product was being shipped out, as it had been for the last twenty years, but nobody was buying. The American public, after being taken vicariously to Stalingrad, Iwo Jima, Buchenwald and Potsdam, was suddenly disenchanted about taking itself to the Bijou or Orpheum twice a week, come rain, shine or Kay Francis. . . . They were also mightily intrigued by a new home appliance called television." Hollywood passed the rest of the decade in a dither, trying 3-D, wide screen, serious pictures, unserious pictures, big pictures, small pictures, searching for the magic formula that would restore its health.

Les girls HEDY LAMARR

Miss Lamarr before Hollywood (in Ecstasy—*when she was still a teen-ager)* . . .

HEDY LAMARR, ACCORDING TO one reputable film history, was "the only big new star to emerge at the end of the thirties." She was a woman of transcendent beauty and, apparently, of some wit. "Any girl can be glamorous," she is reputed to have said. "All you have to do is stand still and look stupid." Miss Lamarr had absolutely no peer at this occupation and, following her American debut in *Algiers* (1938), with its famous line, "Come wiz me to the Casbah," she became, during the forties, the reigning symbol of mysterious womanhood. Although her enigma was not so deep as Garbo's, there is no doubt that she exercised some measure of a similar appeal. Parker Tyler declared: "Miss Lamarr doesn't have to say 'Yes,' all she has to do is yawn. . . . In her perfect will-lessness Miss Lamarr is, indeed,

identified *metaphysically* with her mesmeric midnight captor, the loving male."

But there was a little bit more to Miss Lamarr than that. For, ironically, this masklike beauty belonged to a young woman who, in 1931, had gamboled nude before the cameras for an avant-garde (and perfectly dreadful) film called *Ecstasy*. She had been little more than a post-nymphet at the time of her famous run through the woods and her dip in a sylvan pool, but the fact that she had done so gave her a spurious wickedness. Perhaps, one thought watching her, there was more here than met the eye. Alas, there was probably less, but in the war years she symbolized a downbeat exoticism.

and after. She plays Joan of Arc in a multistar history of civilization as it looked from the film capital.

Ann Sheridan does her bit for publicity.

Les girls PIN-UPS

IN WORLD WAR II WE FOUGHT for—along with our right to boo the Dodgers—the right to worship the American girl. Her altar was the barracks wall, and on it her image, in a thousand varieties, was pinned up. The intellectuals might understand, as Elizabeth Hardwick phrased it, that "this naïve, friendly surface is a disguise . . . a marvelous baroque invention masking a soul shriveled by Puritanism and a vanity swollen by leisure and power." But under stress, the ordinary American male discovered that he missed her terribly, this "informal, independent, lively" child-woman and since she could not be with him in battle, the movies, in a burst of patriotism, provided him with literally thousands of images of her.

The pin-up was a curiously sexless creation, neither vamp nor virgin. The question of her real sexual proclivities was rarely raised. She simply existed to remind the absent male of woman as woman. He could invest the image with any qualities he personally admired. The result, as far as Hollywood was concerned, was a crop of girls with no striking—or durable—characteristics at all. Most of them faded quickly when the war ended, although some may still be found working in road companies, in summer stock or simply as "celebrities," known for their "well-knownness," as one commentator put it.

Of them all, Paulette Goddard was the most appealing. Chaplin had spotted the one-time Ziegfeld girl when she was working for Hal Roach as a bit player, and he cast her as the gamine in *Modern Times.* They were married secretly and for one amusing year refused to confirm or deny the fact. Chaplin's son, recalling the first time he and his brother met her, says, "Syd and I lifted our heads and looked into that friendly face with its mischievous, conspiratorial smile and we lost our hearts at once, never to regain them through all the golden years of our childhood." Miss Goddard did not retain the affection of Chaplin—or of the public—for very long. She divorced Chaplin, and by the early fifties she was out of films. In a way it was too bad. Hers was a spirited, spunky presence and she asserted something like a genuine personality at a time when it was difficult to do so.

Ann Sheridan was a less individualized creation. She arrived in Hollywood from Texas in 1933, winner of a "search for beauty" contest. The *oomph* girl's career was little more than a collection of publicity stills until *King's Row* (1941) established her as a player of some importance. Throughout the forties she appeared mainly in comedies and musicals, then she, too, disappeared from the front rank of film stars.

Lana Turner managed to avoid that fate. She, of course, was the most famous of the drugstore discoveries. Perched on a soda fountain stool, she was asked the time-honored question: "How would you like to be in pictures?" and Mervyn Leroy cast her in a bit part as the girl who was murdered in the first reel of *They Won't Forget,* an antilynching drama of 1937. Clad in a tight sweater, Miss Turner bounced to fame in mere minutes of screen time. By 1941 she was a star. Her career dimmed in the fifties, but she has made a strong comeback in films which ask whether a woman over forty can find happiness. She has learned to suffer beautifully, and richly tearful future beckons.

Paulette Goddard manages to look fetching despite the rags and dirt of Kitty *before her rise to riches and power.*

Lana Turner in The Prodigal, which was prodigal in its waste of screen time, Metro's money.

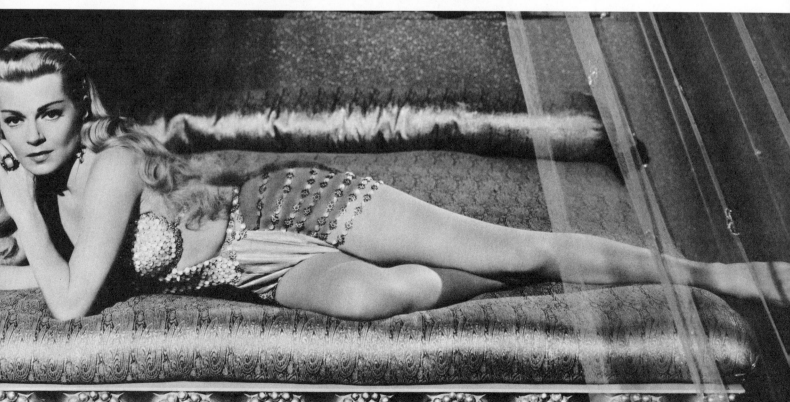

Les girls
AND MORE PIN-UPS

THE MISSES LAMOUR AND GRABLE were undoubtedly the top pin-up girls of World War II, the latter having a slight edge in popularity. She was, for four years, the leading box-office attraction of the movies. Her special forte was the backstage musical in which her famous legs were put on display on the most absurd of pretexts. Miss Grable's beauty—if that is the word for it—was of the common sort. Nor did she offer much in the way of character or maturity. She was, at best, a sort of great American floozie, and her appeal to lonely GI's was surely that of every hash-house waitress with whom they had ever flirted.

Miss Lamour, on the other hand, was first offered as a unique type—a bird of paradise, if you will. Since it was impossible for her to deliver a line with any inflection other than that of a child doing a recitation, she was shrewdly cast as a monosyllabic South Seas seductress, wild and untamed until someone like Jon Hall hove onto the scene.

A former elevator operator, Miss Lamour had been crowned Miss New Orleans of 1931 and was a band singer before going to Hollywood. She found her métier as foil to Bob Hope and Bing Crosby in the *Road* pictures, where her costume—the sarong—was as before, but her character became rather breezy and brash.

The two of them, Grable and Lamour, represented democratic womanhood's lowest common denominator. It is not surprising that they reached the heights of popularity in a nation at war to protect democratic values, or that once the crisis passed and there was time for the finer things they disappeared from view with hardly a trace.

Miss Grable appears in Coney Island, *Miss Lamour has hung her sarong on the line—just outside the publicity department—to dry.*

The girl as goddess RITA HAYWORTH

Gene Kelly, Rita Hayworth, Phil Silvers, in Cover Girl. *Jerome Kern wrote the music.*

WHEN HE CAME TO WRITE his justly famed 1947 *Life* study "The Cult of the Love Goddess in America," Winthrop Sargeant focused his attention on Miss Rita Hayworth, then the reigning deity. "The fundamental trait of Rita's character is simply the desire to please people," he wrote. "She is almost the perfect embodiment of that quality of passivity which poets, in more classically minded times, thought of as the essence of the female nature. Like the ideal, theoretical woman, Rita exerts enormous power by merely existing. She causes or inspires action, but she does not act herself, except in response to the desires of others."

Pointing out that Rita stood at the center of a "heroic industrial operation," Sargeant found it amazing that she was "a rather likable, simple and completely unaffected human being." Temperamentally placid, extremely shy, she seemed to him to have as her chief aim in life a desire to carry out, letter-perfect, the instructions of the many people who had taken a hand in creating, out of this daughter of a family of Spanish dancers, a symbol of sensuality so potent that her likeness was affixed to the first atomic bomb the United States tested after World War II. The "ideal mix-

ture of American girlish health with just a teasing trace of Latin dignity and feline exoticism," Miss Hayworth was lost in the B-picture jungles until her first husband, a car salesman, began her exploitation. She got some good roles, then confirmed her position in Fred Astaire musicals and, finally, in *Cover Girl,* a fine, funny musical of the forties. *Gilda,* a melodrama in which she was uninhibitedly erotic, added just the right dash of spice to her public image.

Her marriage to Aly Kahn halted the development of her career, and in the early fifties she was replaced as our leading love object. In recent years, however, she has returned to films. There are circles under her eyes now, and an indefinable sadness about her presence. She seems, on screen, to be a woman who has seen too much, lived too hard. There is about her the nobility of a splendid ruin glimpsed in twilight, and if anything, she is more delicious than ever. She had been the greatest girl of them all, a living summary of all our sexy, dreamy ideals. Now she is a reminder, for an aging generation, of the generous visions of youth.

Gilda, *made in 1946 when Rita reigned supreme as the American love goddess.*

Greer Garson and Margaret O'Brien
THE BRAVE ONES

Madame Curie bears up after discovering her husband has radium poisoning.

ALL WAS NOT ESCAPISM in the films of the early forties. Both sentiment and heroism were also present in great measure, and two actresses made careers out of combining those qualities. Both were English and both were, in their ways, more than usually talented.

Greer Garson was discovered by Louis B. Mayer, who went to see a London play called *Old Music*, was disappointed that it was not about waltz time in Vienna, but stayed to be impressed by Miss Garson. He signed her, brought her back to Hollywood, but gave her no work. Finally, she returned to England to make a brief, poignant appearance in *Goodbye, Mr. Chips* at M-G-M's English studios. Brought back to Hollywood, she made *Blossoms in the Dust* (in which she played opposite Walter Pidgeon for the first time), then hesitantly accepted the role of *Mrs. Miniver* which Norma Shearer had rejected. That epic of tremble-chinned courage was rushed into release when President Roosevelt, upon seeing it, urged the producers to get it before the public without delay as a morale booster. Miss Garson thereupon entered a long period of enduring, in her various screen families, such normal, everyday vicissitudes as amnesia and radium poisoning. Once the wartime crisis was past, her talent for suffering became less important to Hollywood; but she made a comeback in 1960 playing brave Eleanor Roosevelt in *Sunrise at Campobello*.

Little Margaret O'Brien was a pocket Garson, with this exception: she was an utterly unaffected and naturally charming actress. *Journey for Margaret*, the story of a courageous little war orphan, was her first picture. It was made by the interesting B-picture unit at M-G-M which Dore Schary headed during the war years, producing such unpretentious, goodhearted (and sentimental) films as *Lassie Come Home*, *Joe Smith, American* and *The War Against Mrs. Hadley*. In her best films, like the memorable *Meet Me in St Louis*, which was Hollywood at its slickly sentimental best, Margaret O'Brien presented a perfect vision of the reality of childhood—its frets, humors, even its small neuroses. "She is an uncannily talented child," wrote James Agee, "and it is infuriating to see her handled, and gradually being ruined, by oafs."

Journey for Margaret *was the beginning of Margaret O'Brien's journey to fame*

Johnson in Command Decision.

VAN JOHNSON

IF GREER GARSON REPRESENTED the free world's ideal mother in the war years, and Margaret O'Brien its idealization of childhood innocence, then Van Johnson and June Allyson, who were frequently costarred, represented our ideal of promising youth. Both of them broke into show business in the choruses of Broadway musicals and both of them had a fresh-faced charm, a soft edge of naïvety, and a wide-open honesty in their presences.

Johnson made his first movie in 1941, emerged as a star of great teen-age appeal (he was called "The Voiceless Sinatra") in *The War Against Mrs. Hadley*. A serious auto accident scarred his forehead deeply and almost ended his career abruptly. Spencer Tracy saved it by insisting that the picture they were then working on, *A Guy Named Joe*, be held up until he recovered. His brush with death seemed, briefly, to enhance his career, but unfortunately, and ironi-

The girl next door

Allyson in The Stratton Story.

cally, his audience outgrew him. They aged, but he did not seem to. Declaring that he had been a movie star and now very much wanted to be an actor, he insisted that "a man just gets to his beautiful period when he is forty." His trouble was that when he reached that age he did not look appreciably different than he had at twenty, and so he had trouble sustaining belief in his maturity, despite excellent portrayals (Marek in *The Caine Mutiny*, for instance).

Miss Allyson faced a similar problem, surmounted it by playing the grown-up-and-married version of her former screen self, then brought her vaunted sweetness to the part of the venomous bitch of *The Shrike*. It was a delicious combination—her surface sweetness and the inner viciousness of the role. A woman who genuinely dislikes being a star, she has not pursued the new career that this role might have opened for her.

JUNE ALLYSON

Two for the road BOB HOPE

Bob Hope and friend in The Road to Morocco.

BOB HOPE IS THE MAN who adapted the principles of the assembly line to the production of humor. He turns out a standardized product—topical wisecracks—in a rapid-fire stream. There is nothing very elegant about the product; it lacks the intricate charm of humor that is carefully hand-crafted to express a highly individual point of view. But it is a miracle of sheer volume, and in each string of gags there is usually at least one that has a seemingly accidental perfection.

Like a machine, Hope maintains a perfectly neutral relationship with his environment. It exists only to provide him with "material" which he efficiently and unemotionally processes. It is impossible to tell from his jokes what—if anything—he really values or really loathes. He lays about him with a fine impartiality. His sallies are completely without passion. Ironically, he is therefore able to get away with more cruelty in his wit than a comedian who invests his humor with a more personal feeling.

So far as his public is concerned, Hope is a man without roots or human ties. No major celebrity of our time has more successfully separated his public existence from his private life. His sketchy biography tells us he was born in England, grew up in Cleveland, entered show business as a dancer, spent long, lean years in the lower levels of vaudeville, switched to comedy somewhere along the line and achieved his first success in Broadway musicals. Radio—a medium that was made for his style—was next; then movies, starting with *The Big Broadcast* of 1938.

Undoubtedly his finest hour occurred during World War II, and it is possible that when the definitive social history of that war is written, Hope will be recognized as representative of what was best in America's response to crisis. With no thought of a cost-plus contract, he put his joke factory to work for the government, providing his special brand of civilian-type humor for men who were suddenly, shockingly not civilians any more but who welcomed a reminder that they had been and wanted to be again. Hope has never explained why he undertook his program of good work. Like his humor, it simply came to exist, a surprising *beau geste* from a man who has managed the remarkable trick of being funny without ever revealing his true self.

Bob Hope and friend in That Certain Feeling.

...and BING CROSBY

BING CROSBY, TOO, simply exists. He is not so interesting a personality as Bob Hope, for there is nothing enigmatic about him. The open, comfortable, relaxed, unpretentious public personality is apparently a true reflection of the man himself. One of those performers who simply does what comes naturally to him, he has found that the public is capable of seeing itself in his work. "Bing sings," Dinah Shore once remarked, "like all people think they sing in the shower." In addition, he conducts himself as most people like to think they would behave if they were thrust suddenly into celebrity.

Crosby's history is well known. He gave up his studies at Gonzaga University in order to sing, because singing was what he most enjoyed doing. He and a friend caught on with the Paul Whiteman band, leaving a trail of empty bottles and wild oats across the country during the band's tours. Crosby left all that behind him when he married his first wife, Dixie, and became an overnight sensation with his first radio show in 1932. Movie success quickly followed. His career reached a peak in the war years when both in films and on the radio he consistently headed popularity polls, when he won an Academy Award for *Going My Way* and when the *Road* series with Hope was launched and was at its best. They complemented one another. Hope relates best to people in the mass; Crosby on a more intimate basis. The machinelike energy of the one and the casualness of the other are two poles of American character, and they made a spark jump between them. Or, perhaps in tandem each supplies something the other lacks, and two good performers become the equivalent of a single great one.

Crosby the actor. He gave an excellent performance in The Country Girl *(1954), in which charm became weakness.*

Crosby the personality. Star-Spangled Rhythm *was part of a wartime cycle of revues in movie form. Perfectly dreadful as entertainment, their proceeds frequently went to aid the war effort.*

Das lied von der erde
INGRID BERGMAN

INGRID BERGMAN'S CHIEF PROBLEM has always been her image. It was, in the beginning, a comparatively simple one, based on the public's obvious associations to the shining healthiness of her appearance. Beyond that, she seemed a rather placid girl with the calmness of simplicity about her, as well as a decent—and rare—kind of earthiness. She was the sort of girl that men think of as the perfect mother for their children. When one looked upon Ingrid Bergman, one saw a woman who would make few demands yet would be instantly, cheerfully responsive to any demands made upon her. There was, the public would learn, a good deal more to Miss Bergman than that, but David O. Selznick carefully built up an image of Bergman as the star without temperament, the actress as homebody.

The orphaned daughter of a _bon vivant_ Stockholm photographer, she had been taunted as a child because of her clumsiness; she became an actress in school productions "because then I'm not myself." After high school she entered the Swedish Royal Academy and, visiting a friend on a movie lot, was discovered by a director and a producer who were looking for a leading lady for a film called _The Surf._ A colleague from her early days of quick success in Swedish movies recalls that "she always radiated phenomenal health, strength and vitality," that she had "iron will power and an unbelievable memory."

After a four-year courtship, she married Peter Lindstrom, a dentist who eventually became a brain surgeon. Shortly thereafter, she went to Hollywood, where Selznick remade one of her Swedish successes, _Intermezzo,_ then loaned her out for the series of films (_Rage in Heaven, Dr. Jekyll and Mr. Hyde, Casablanca, For Whom the Bell Tolls, Saratoga Trunk, Gaslight_) that established her, in the early forties, both as an actress of considerable talent and as a personality

Ingrid Bergman's first American movie was Intermezzo, _a remake of one of her Swedish successes. Producer David Selznick thought a familiar role would build her confidence._ Saratoga Trunk _(1945) was a movie with a theme as non-Swedish as you can get._

229

who radiated mental health, high morality and, for that matter, all the virtues of the balanced life.

Her career and marriage both soured somewhat as the decade wore on. The former peaked with her appearance as *Joan of Lorraine* on Broadway. Significantly, Joan was her favorite saint, and with her Miss Bergman shared certain significant traits—physical strength, personal integrity, driving ambition, a disconcerting habit of speaking the truth, a way of angering less generous spirits. At any rate, she broke with Selznick, made three disastrous flops (including another portrayal of Joan, this time in an ill-conceived film). At the same time her marriage was encountering difficulties. Her career and that of her husband were increasingly divergent. Restless and unhappy, she saw the films of Roberto Rossellini, was impressed, and wrote him a letter, offering to work for him. Rossellini's neo-realistic films—first of the postwar European movies to catch the American eye—were not the finest of their type, but they did have a certain power, especially for an actress who was bored with the overwrought phoniness of the Hollywood product and who probably sensed the need for a change in type.

In any case, she was soon making the wretched *Stromboli* in Italy. Without a studio's press agents to protect her reputation, her romance with Rossellini flamed on the front pages. On the floor of the United States Senate she was called "a free-love cultist," "Hollywood's apostle of degradation" and "a powerful influence for evil." Ostracized from the American movie community, she was not rehabilitated in public favor until Rossellini went off to India to embark on a film and another overpublicized romance. Just then Twentieth Century Fox took a chance on Bergman for the lead in *Anastasia,* and when she returned to this country after that film, Ed Sullivan polled his viewers as to whether, in effect, Miss Bergman had been punished enough and whether they would like to see her on his television program. The mail ran against her, but majority opinion, outraged by the vulgarity of the poll, began to swing in her favor.

Now, nearing fifty, Miss Bergman has married again—this time to an enterprising Swedish businessman. She is a more matronly figure, and her appeal is considerably different from what it was. She has the honest sensuality of what the French call "a woman of a certain age." Her presence suggests worldly experience and hunger for a new romantic truth, both informed by a wryly amused acceptance of the way things are. "She dares to live truthfully," says Gary Grant, and in her maturity, Ingrid Bergman is an infinitely more interesting screen figure than she was in her fresh-faced youth.

Bergman and Cooper in For Whom the Bell Tolls.

A touch of elegance
CARY GRANT

DAVID NIVEN THINKS CARY GRANT is "a spooky Celt really, not an Englishman at all. Must be some fey Welsh blood there someplace." Grant's style is based on faultless grace and elegance, and thus he represents the distilled essence of one—but only one—of the ideal qualities the American woman would like to find in her mate. It is a quality that is particularly rare in the domestic male and one which he contends is rather sissified. It may be described as easy charm. Grant provides it for the ladies and at the same time seems to kid it, thus making his screen self palatable to men as well. The fact that he is not to the manner born probably helps to make his double-edged portrayals easier for him.

Grant was born into a family of modest circumstances in Bristol, England. His mother suffered a mental breakdown when he was twelve, and his father sought solace with another woman, by whom he had a child. Grant shortly joined a juvenile acrobatic troupe, whose wandering existence suited his restlessness. Eventually he came to New York, worked in musical comedies, then went to Hollywood to play bits. Mae West spotted him on the Paramount lot and, since there was always room for someone of his type in her films, cast him in his first leading role. The picture was *She Done Him Wrong*, the screen version of her stage success *Diamond Lil*.

"I became an actor for the usual reasons," Grant has recalled, "a great need to be liked and admired. Besides, picture making is adventurous." He has been at it for almost thirty years now, and one of the most remarkable things about him is utter agelessness. In effect, he is still playing juveniles. He owes this to various forms of rigorous self-discipline and, he claims, to psychotherapy. Whatever accounts for it, there is no doubt that the Grant screen character is built on a solid foundation. In parts that could easily become foppish and foolish in less skilled hands, there is always a suggestion of inner strength which makes believable the "wary rapacity" with which he approaches his leading ladies.

A cold, humorous tub in The Howards of Virginia.

233

Grant at his ever youthful best in Indiscreet.

JOHN WAYNE *The unacclaimed hero*

A change of pace for Wayne. He plays (opposite Maureen O'Hara) in The Quiet Man, *John Ford's salty tribute to the Ould Sod.*

AMONG THE FINER SENSIBILITIES who are fond of movies, there has never been much feeling for John Wayne. His conservative politics are anathema to those liberal intellectuals who have concerned themselves with film; the flat accents of his voice, his lumbering movements, have never commended him to connoisseurs either of acting or of male beauty. He is, apparently, loved only by the people who, since he rose from the grade-Z Westerns that he made in the early thirties, have made him one of the all-time box-office champions.

What they see in him is a screen personality who is dully, stupidly, triumphantly and, without the slightest subtlety, 100-per-cent American male. Wayne, who has a hero-worshiping admiration for director John Ford, has frequently said that the director taught him not acting but reacting. Thus a Wayne film is usually a curious phenomenon. The star stands at its dead center, still as the eye of a hurricane, while around him forces of tremendous magnitude are unloosed. The fun lies in watching him bring his remarkable physical strength and technical know-how into play against these forces.

Wayne's character has no inner resonance. Cooper's Westerner, for example, could be imagined philosophizing about his relationship with his environment. Wayne is never truly at ease with it; he lacks any capacity to give himself to it. It is for this reason that his best Western roles have been as cavalry officers, men who live in the wilderness not through choice but because they have been ordered to do

"Everybody gets dead." The name of the film is Hondo.

so. Wayne's Western knowledge thus seems to have been acquired under compulsion, rather than as a natural part of growing up. It is no less valid for that reason, and it is nonsense to question his proficiency in such matters as tracking, horsemanship and Indian psychology. What is interesting about Wayne is his very awkwardness, the slight feeling of unease, for which he compensates by being more aggressively masculine than other Western stars. He is, for instance, ruder with women than the others, a little tougher on the tenderfoot or the juvenile. The bark of his commanding voice seems a little harsher than that of his rivals, the impact of his avenging fists a little sharper.

All this undoubtedly results from the fact that Wayne is by no means a natural actor. The unease of his character may be nothing more than that of a man made uncomfortable by having his picture taken.

He was a football star at the University of Southern Cali-

fornia and worked for Ford as a prop boy in the summers. Ford gave him some small parts, which led to the quickie Western career from which, in time, Ford rescued him by giving him the lead in the memorable *Stagecoach*. "I made so many pictures in the early days, I couldn't begin to tell you how many I was in," says Wayne. "I made a lot of those four- and five-day westerns designed for kids. I built a young audience with those, and the kids grew up and started going to see me in more adult things. Also, during the past ten years, they've been showing my old quickies on television, and they've given me a whole new audience of kids—children of the ones who went to see me in the first place. . . . It's constant exposure that builds you up as a personality." At any rate, following his success in *Stagecoach*, the lead in *Reap the Wild Wind*, a DeMille spectacle of 1940, solidified Wayne's position, and during the war years Wayne emerged as a star of the first rank.

The militarist. He received Academy Award nomination for Sands of Iwo Jima . . .
but was at his best in Fort Apache, *another John Ford production.*

AVA GARDNER *Temporary goddess*

QUIETLY LIBIDINAL AVA GARDNER replaced Rita Hayworth, in the late forties and early fifties, as Hollywood's leading love goddess. She was less sparkly than Rita, and her reign, coming just before Marilyn Monroe's, was a short one, but she had certain symbolic virtues that were not to be denied. She was billed in *The Barefoot Contessa* as "the world's most beautiful animal," and for once the billing was accurate, if not necessarily in its use of the superlative, then in summarizing the spirit of the star. There is indeed an animal quality about her sensuality. She is a proud, prowling, restless tigress, sure of her powers, yet confused about their proper uses.

It is not surprising that Ava Gardner reached her greatest popularity in a period when the nation itself seemed to lose its sense of direction and purpose. For the sum of her characteristics has always been that of slumbering greatness as a love object, not fulfillment. She seems in need of the magic wand that will awaken and synthesize all the qualities which, in various roles, she has evinced. She acts, in short, with the distracted air of a woman searching for something she cannot quite define.

Born in some place called Smithfield, North Carolina, she led an oversheltered, apparently loveless childhood, followed an older sister to New York with vague plans to become a secretary. Her sister's husband was a photographer and he used Ava for a model. An M-G-M scout saw her photo in a shop window and she became first a starlet, then Mickey Rooney's wife. Her first important role was *The Hucksters* (1946), in which she played a "palsy" former lover of hero Clark Gable. There has been something of the pal in most of her portrayals since. She is always the girl who goes to bed with the guy first, then discovers that she loves him. Her approach, you see, is all very modern.

The exotic Ava Gardner as a half-caste Indian in Bhowani Junction.

Mogambo. *Gardner repeated the role Jean Harlow created in* Red Dust *in 1932.*

The triumph of the super-ego
GREGORY PECK

GREGORY PECK IS A HANDY, all-purpose hero whose un-obtrusive presence has, since 1944, adorned a great many expensive, serious, intelligent, but in the last analysis, un-inspired, films. When he made *The Keys of the Kingdom*, James Agee mused on why, at first glance, Peck seemed to be a gifted actor and why that impression faded so quickly. "Now, it seems to me that he probably has talent, in a still semiprofessional stage, and that I was moved and misled rather by his newness, his unusual handsomeness, and his still more unusual ability to communicate sincerity."

Peck has professionalized his talent, but not, of course, as an actor. His profession is stardom, and upon his ability to play sincerity he has based his star personality. It is an extremely appealing one, strong, masculine, honest. He is effective in Westerns and adventure romances but his specialty is the modern, troubled intellectual. In *Gentleman's Agreement*, *The Snows of Kilimanjaro*, *The Man in the Gray Flannel Suit*, *Beloved Infidel* he has played writers whose integrity, either as men or as artists was somehow threatened by the pressures of his time.

Peck's passion never leaps high; it smolders, and when he is called upon to play, for example, Ahab in *Moby Dick*, he cannot quite realize the full-scale emotionality of the role. He is, himself, the thoroughgoing professional, careful of himself, proud of his craft and, like his screen character, rather unegotistical. As a solid pro, Peck has always been careful to pick strong stories, and in no way has he allowed his personality to interfere with their telling. He is, in short, very much the model of modern movie star. His presence is more self-effacing than that of the superstars of the previous generation. He is not bland in the manner of the faceless youths who have been billed as stars in the fifties, but neither is he so engaging an *individual* as his predecessors. A quiet worrier rather than a passionate setter-to-rights, he is an idealized mid-century everyman in a button-down collar.

The white hunter in The Macomber Affair *(1947).*

The Gunfighter. *"A man ought to have more to show for his life than a gold watch."*

THE

PART SEVEN

FIFTIES

ONE DAY EARLY IN 1961, Carl Foreman, an independent motion-picture producer, sat down with New York *Times* reporter Murray Schumach to survey the remains of the once proud and powerful American motion-picture industry. As they talked, one great studio and two or three minor ones had ceased entirely to exist. Another was renting space on the lot it had once owned and later sold to a producer of filmed television shows. Another was busy exploring for oil and subdividing its lot, its fate as a producer dependent on a multimillion-dollar picture, the cost of which had somehow got out of hand and which, unless it turned out to be the biggest hit in history, might well ruin the studio. Not far away, the grandest studio of them all, M-G-M, having almost destroyed itself by clinging too long to the old ways of doing business, had but recently bailed itself out of trouble by producing a smasheroo called *Ben-Hur*, and was now once again in trouble because too much had been spent remaking a former hit, *Mutiny on the Bounty*.

Such has been the caliber of Hollywood industrial statesmanship that it was characteristic of Metro to remake old successes in an attempt to survive rather than to think up something new to do. It was to this general softening of the brain that Mr. Foreman was hyperbolically addressing himself. "The movie business in Hollywood," he said, "is the only business in the history of the United States that set out to destroy itself. . . . It is the only business where the men at the top discharged or devoured all the younger men who could have carried on. Hollywood today is in a complete state of anarchy.

"What they have," he continued, "is an ever-decreasing number of stars getting ever-increasing salaries. This is insane." Asserting that it was healthy for movie making to go out into the great world and break out of the confining studio walls, he suggested that the industry might need government subsidies and a training school for new talent. "The bulk of Hollywood movies are old-fashioned and creaky," he declared. "There is nothing here to compare with the ferment in Great Britain, France or even Poland, which is behind the Iron Curtain."

Many things besides television have contributed to the decline of Hollywood in the postwar years. The nation was spending its leisure hours in different ways—in do-it-yourself projects around home, in travel, in self-improvement, in community activities, in God-knows-what. There were, simply, far more demands on the average citizen's time than there once had been, and he had more money and education to spend on more elaborate cultural pursuits than a Saturday night at the movies. In addition, the importation of foreign films, as well as Hollywood's own occasional forays into the realm of genuine art, had convinced him that movies should be something more than a habit, that they could be, at their best, an experience, and that he was quite within his rights to be choosy about them—especially when his longing for trash could be so easily satisfied at home by the mere flick of a switch.

For those who were adaptable there were still fortunes to be made in the Hollywood of the fifties. The operational principle was to avoid getting yourself tied up "in concrete," as the saying went. The old Hollywood had, indeed, been set up on industrial lines. Movies were interchangeable products—like cans of corn—and you moved as many cans as possible off the shelves and into the stores each year. If you lost money on one line of products, you were sure to make it up on another. The main thing was production. This, of course, entailed a heavy overhead. Assembly lines cost money to establish and to operate; they require much "concrete." The new Hollywood discovered that with fewer theaters in operation (and television forced the marginal ones out of business very quickly) it needed much less product than it once had. With less product needed, it discovered that it needed less "concrete," and far fewer employees. Even some of the moguls' relatives lost their jobs.

After much stumbling about in a wilderness of conflicting advice, and many yelping runs down false trails, the movie makers began to operate within a new industrial pattern which emerged by the middle of the decade. The old-line studios became, in effect, real estate operators, loan sharks and comparatively passive distributors of other people's products. They rented their production facilities, loaned money to and distributed the product of independent packagers of various types. Some of these were former employees —directors, stars, even staff producers—who knew how to write their names or, even better, how to talk awfully fast, and who whirled around town, wrapping "packages" which could be converted into cash for production. They started with a "property," then interested a guaranteed superstar in appearing in the movie version. With him lined up, yet another and another and another could be brought into camp. Add a director and a screenwriter along the way, and the moguls became as children, eager to press money on the operator.

Now it quickly became obvious that the key to all this was the star. He could not just be anybody who had once had his name billed above a picture's title. He had to be somebody who, on the form charts, could bring the people in. There were very few such gilt-edged drawing cards in the business, and most of them quickly incorporated themselves and learned to wrap their own packages. This happy few could be lured into other people's pictures, but it came to be considered *declassé*, if not downright vulgar, to "take money." What one takes, ideally, is a percentage of a film's gross. Second best is a percentage of the profits—which most studios prefer, since 50 per cent of nothing is still nothing, while 10 per cent of a film's gross, even when that gross does not return the cost of making the negative, can be considerable. Obviously there is little long-term security for the star

in such a system. He therefore charges what the traffic will bear and there are now signs that the money men are about to revolt against the heavy duties the stars have lately exacted. The handful of stars who have survived and prospered may, in the immediate future, face a dowward revision of the prices they can get.

But at last the importance of the star, and to a lesser degree that of directors and writers, is being recognized. This is not only stated in terms of remuneration, but in terms of status. They—or at any rate their agents and managers— are calling the shots now, and as a result they are acquiring something at least as satisfying to the ego as publicity— membership in the real power elite of Hollywood.

The results of the big change-over are interestingly mixed. The easy money has virtually disappeared, and that is good. So is the disappearance of the arrogant, unbridled power of the studios. Something like a free market place has begun to exist in Hollywood today. There are many buyers and many sellers of talent, ideas and money, and the old dominance of a handful of tycoons is almost finished.

With production spread among so many small companies, the threat of boycott is lessened and pressure groups are denied the leverage they once had on the studios, which dared not threaten their entire output to protect a single controversial film. Because the public apparently wants more adult pictures, and because creative people are finally free to indulge themselves in ideas that would have been vetoed by the frightened Philistines of the old-time front office, films have a new seriousness about them.

But, there are "buts." To begin with, there is no American art film tradition. Cast off from the rigid disciplines of studio-style production, many would-be film artists flounder. They have toiled too long under the old way of doing business and they find, now that they may speak freely, that they can, alas, only talk in the old accents. Many of them were not very fine minds to begin with, and their attempts at seriousness are more laughable—and far less entertaining—than were the standardized items they used to grind out. Many of the new talents are more pretentious than portentous.

While the new independence has given us much that is arty, the percentage of the product that is genuine art is not much higher than it ever was; and, remember, the total number of films produced is smaller. In addition, there is an increasing reliance on the superspectacle, frequently Biblical or historical in theme; and these, though often profitable, are even more often regressive as screen art. Then, too, there is a greater reliance on the pre-sold property, the best-selling book or hit play or, as we have seen, the previously success-

James Dean's career covered just a few years of the fifties, but his brooding, withdrawn, rebellious, sensitive presence struck a particularly responsive chord during the decade—especially among the young audiences.

ful film, and so the percentage of original screenplays, in which lies whatever hope there is for the creation of a uniquely American screen art, dwindles. Too many recent films are merely expensive and stupid mountings of properties that should never have been translated to the screen.

Finally, and this is most germane to the history of movie stardom, no one is building for the future in Hollywood. The studios, for all their terrible faults and without doing all they should have done, had the resources and the economic self-interest to try to develop new talent. As we have seen, it takes as many as ten years for a star to develop his full potential, and in the process there has to be room for considerable trial and error, plus the resources to carry those failures which are an inevitable byproduct of such a process. The independents, concerned with just one film at a time, and the immediate profit or loss which will determine their ability to make another film, do not have the time, resources or inclination to worry about such matters. For them the future stretches no farther ahead than next year.

The studios, most of whom keep a few youngsters under contract, are frankly worried about more pressing matters than the stars of the next decade. For them there may be no next decade anyway. So, it is very difficult, under present conditions, to learn the trade of stardom. Growth is forced,

and there are not enough unimportant films in which to test talents. One remembers how many stars, writers and directors Metro harvested from its B-picture units (and, incidentally, how many of the little pictures were infinitely better than the big ones), and one despairs of Hollywood's future. The irony is that television may be the modern equivalent of the old B film, the farm system for new talent. Meantime, careers are lasting so long that many of them are being ended, remarkably, by natural causes, by the diseases that aging flesh is heir to.

Of one thing, however, we may be certain. The cult of personality is deeply imbedded in our attitudes toward films. It is true that, today more than ever before, films—especially foreign films—can be commercial successes without stars. But the irony is that the public, just as it did in the time when there were no such things as stars, quickly picks out the most interesting faces in these films and insists on knowing more about them. The human need for stars seems to remain, for good or ill, constant. The public may be plucking fewer new stars from the backgrounds of American movies, but it is finding them elsewhere—on the stage, in television, in movies made abroad—and is forcing them on the American movie maker.

Alan Ladd maintains his composure, even during the epochal brawl in Sh

THE BLAND BLONDE has always been something of a sta in Hollywood, but diminutive Alan Ladd is probably the t male star to achieve fame by combining beauty and s nambulism like the female of the species. So unemotic was he, with his deadness of voice and feature, that in sc movies he succeeded in reducing murder to an act as relevant as crossing the street. By this absence of emotio created a wonderful commentary on violence. Similarly, frozen good looks could be read as a symbol of evil's oj site, as in *Shane*. But he was an actor singularly depend since he was a symbol rather than a human being, on

THE SOMNAMBULISTS

Kim Novak remained triumphantly somnambulistic, even when playing a witch.

taste and abilities of his directorial manipulators, and so his vogue was very brief. *Shane* was his last important picture.

Like Ladd, Kim Novak, his female counterpart, is utterly dependent on her manipulators. Her career, which began in the early fifties when Ladd's began to taper off, is already on the wane. Says producer Jerry Wald: "Generally these kids come from poor or lower-middle-class backgrounds. Generally they're terribly insecure and only half formed as individuals when we get them. They're still asking themselves, 'Who am I? What am I?' Then, overnight, they're stars. Their development as individuals becomes arrested be-

cause suddenly we're making all the decisions for them and they don't have to think much. So they remain like children, still trying to discover their true personality. . . ."

The essence of the female somnambulist's appeal is that the male in the audience dreams he can become her master. Their tragedy is that they have, in fact, been mastered and are therefore denied the opportunity to learn how to be people—and it is as people, not as symbols, that the stars survive. In the faceless fifties, however, as one psychiatrist put it, the dehumanized stars "go well with an era that suffers from a loss of identity."

WILLIAM HOLDEN

William Holden, Gloria Swanson, in Sunset Boulevard, *the film which rescued his career.*

IN 1949, WILLIAM HOLDEN told an interviewer that he liked to make three kinds of movies—Westerns, "because they keep me outside, give me lots of exercise"; comedies, "because they're the ones that bring money into the box office"; and serious dramas, because "I hope maybe some day a critic will spot me and say 'Aha, *that's* the boy!'"

Discovered in a student dramatics group at South Pasadena Junior College, he became a star in 1939 as the fighter-fiddler in *Golden Boy*, made a few pictures that established him as a promising Boy Next Door, then went into the Army. After the war, he played a succession of similar parts and found that he was just another standard hero, indistinguishable from William Lundigan or Dennis O'Keefe or any of a dozen other profiles whose names are already half forgotten. But a year after his somewhat wistful statement, critics, producers and public were saying "Aha," because Billy Wilder had cast him as the gigolo to Gloria Swanson's aging movie queen in *Sunset Boulevard*. Four years later he won an Oscar for his

tough, funny con man in Wilder's *Stalag 17*. Ever since, he has been ranked as a superstar, one of those who disdain to accept "just money."

Like Peck, his off-screen demeanor is that of a bright young corporation president, whose product is himself. But there is an edge of anger, or perhaps just wildness (he does his own stunts) about him. One shrewd friend has said, "He's the typical American boy who wanted to become a slob—and never did." Adds Wilder, "Only actors who are ashamed to act are worth their salt. . . . Anybody who tears himself to shreds being hammy, I suspect. That's why I'm fond of Holden. He dies every time he has to act. . . . He's beyond acting. He is there. It is as simple as that. You never doubt or question what he is." Holden, thus became the heir, in the fifties, to the mantle of the great American leading men. Salty yet urbane, he was especially effective in a time which likes a *soupçon* of cynicism in the heroic mix.

The Golden Boy as Golden Boy.
In Holden's first movie, the changeless
Lee J. Cobb played his father.

Holden's All-American good looks lent special irony to his portrayal of a con man in Stalag 17.

Osteopath heal thyself! Burt Lancaster in Come Back, Little Sheba.

BURT LANCASTER, WITH HOLDEN, was the other important leading-man find of the fifties. A lower East Side kid, he had spent the prewar years as a circus acrobat, came out of the Army and made his only Broadway foray in a short-lived play which brought him a movie contract. His first picture, *The Killers* (1946), established him as a star of considerable strength. More than types like Holden, his magnetism was based on sheer—almost brutish—physical force. But he is apparently an actor who is very, very serious about the social value of his trade, as well as a shrewd producer. Both in his selection of roles and in his productions, he has generally opted for the serious, the consciously important theme. Among the first stars to set up his own production company (in 1948), he is at his best in roles that call for outward force (*From Here to Eternity, Sweet Smell of Success, Elmer Gantry*) rather than inner conflict. He has trouble playing intellectuals; but, oddly, his acting technique is cerebral rather than emotional in method. He is best when he does not have to force an emotion. Under such stress he shows too many teeth.

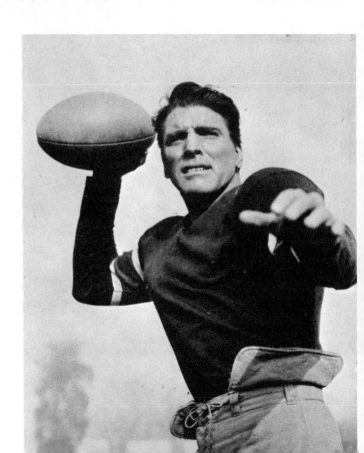

Burt Lancaster, *All-American.*

m Thorpe, All-American.

I Confess. *Hitchcock's study of a priest who discovers, in the confessional, whodunit*

Montgomery Clift, along with Marlon Brando, represented something entirely new on the screen—the inwardly troubled hero. Before them, no one had thought to place before the public a hero with internal problems. The problems faced by their predecessors had to be external—a moral choice, a problem in the technique of getting what you wanted. With Clift and Brando, the age of psychology came to the world of the movie star. Brando, of course, is a more powerful actor, his violence quotient is much higher. But Clift has his points. He is, very simply, more handsome than Brando. And, in addition, he has a reedlike quality; it seems as if he might easily be broken by the forces aligned against him. He has yet to break on the screen, but it always seems a live possibility—more so than it ever has in the work of other male stars.

As a troubled, yet beautifully youthful man, Clift has brought out the mother in a generation of American women who have learned to respond to his special blend of delicacy and resilience. Not surprisingly, many a young matron has been heard to mourn for the lost perfection of his beauty, which was marred in an auto accident. Yet all of them admire the dogged courage with which he has come back from the accident and which usually illuminates—through contrast—his screen portrayals of troubled youth.

The new sensitivity
MONTGOMERY CLIFT

Clift plays the Adventurer in The Heiress *with Olivia De Havilland.*

Clift came to films in 1948, when he made *The Search*, Fred Zinnemann's movingly simple story of the plight of Europe's war orphans. In the same year he made *Red River*, Howard Hawkes's bruising, gritty Western; and it might be said that in Clift's epochal brawl with John Wayne the new Hollywood man fought it out with the old. Significantly, it ended in a draw, but Clift was a star from that point on.

Star status had been a long time coming, for he had begun his acting career in 1935, at fifteen, as a stage juvenile and had appeared thereafter in a number of rather distinguished plays, including *There Shall Be No Night* and *The Skin of Our Teeth*. As reticent as his screen character, and as enigmatic,

Clift has frequently turned down roles because, he says, he wants to be an actor not a star. "I don't have a big urge to act. I can't play something I'm not interested in. If I'm not interested, how can I expect the audience to be."

Unlike Brando, he makes no claim to being a method actor, and he says he works strictly on instinct. "An actor," he has said, "must share experiences familiar to the audience. Otherwise you're making faces in a vacuum." It is hard to know, specifically, what experiences he has shared with the younger generation who made him their own in the fifties, but he does project, with rare fidelity, their inner tensions, the result of rebelliousness suppressed.

The new sensitivity
MARLON
BRANDO

THE FIRST MOVIE MARLON BRANDO MADE was *The Men,* in 1950. Cast as an embittered paraplegic, he endured a month in a hospital ward with men who really had been paralyzed as a result of war wounds. With his usual intensity, Brando experienced the paraplegic's bedridden existence, practiced his exercises, learned to manipulate a wheel chair. Then, one Saturday, he went with some of his ward mates to a beer joint to which they frequently repaired. There they were set upon by a religious fanatic who told them that if they would but have faith they might rise up and walk again. On and on he droned, until Brando cried, "You really mean I can walk if I want to enough?" Not waiting for a reply, he leaped from his chair and dashed from the bar, returning quickly with a bundle of newspapers which he proceeded to hawk up and down the bar, yelling joyously, "Now I can make a living again." The men in the wheel chairs roared with laughter, and if there had been any strain between them and the actors who were suddenly living among them for purposes of the picture, it was ended.

The story is not set down here as an idle anecdote, for it tells a great deal about Marlon Brando—his impatience with the fraudulent, and the open rebellion it causes in him; his uncanny sense of what is natural, what is "right" in the actor's imitation of human behavior; and, perhaps most important of all, his sense of exactly what an audience will accept. One may set aside the fact that his performance in the bar served a good end, the freeing of brave men from tedium, false pity and offensiveness. But it is hard to set aside the fact that Brando's response was very much in the vein of his time, a time which has found Holden Caulfield to be a true hero, a hero whose chief claim upon us is his withering contempt for the phony.

Brando is not liked by the older generation, generally speaking. They accuse him of mumbling and scratching, of an unwonted sullenness, of seeming to brood too much and, when not so occupied, of being too violent, too antisocial. All of this, in a way, is true, and in the noisy campaign he has conducted against the *poseurs* of Hollywood it may be that he has created a pose as phony as any he is reacting against. But its roots lie in an honest reaction. "In my own

behavior with people, if I didn't trust or like someone I
would either say nothing or mumble. I got to be awfully
good at mumbling." His sister Jocelyn reported that he so
desperately wanted honesty that "when somebody was
blatantly dishonest, Marlon was so disappointed he couldn't
talk, he couldn't cope with it, he was too emotional."

It is the honesty of this attitude that illuminates his acting.
Clift may play an inwardly troubled male with equal skill
on occasion, but he remains clean-cut, well dressed. Brando
does not look well dressed even when, in fact, he is. His
features are an odd combination of sensitivity and brutality.
He has eyes, as he once phrased it, "like those of a dead
pig." The natural line of his mouth is a scowly droop, his
hair has been receding for years, and his figure tends toward
the paunchy. These very imperfections enhance the honesty
of his portrayals, reinforce the qualities he is most interested
in examining as an actor.

Brando repeated for the screen the stage role that had
brought him fame, Stanley Kowalski in *A Streetcar Named
Desire.* As Brando played him, Stanley had a certain animal
fascination, but he was undoubtedly repugnant to many
people, even to Brando. "Kowalski was always right, and
never afraid," Brando has said. "He never wondered, he
never doubted. His ego was very secure. And he had the
kind of brutal aggressiveness I hate. I'm afraid of it. I
detest the character."

It should be borne in mind that in the best of his later
roles—as the motorcycle gang leader in *The Wild One,* as
the Mexican revolutionary in *Viva Zapata,* as, most memo-
rably, the troubled dock-walloper in *On the Waterfront,* even
as the soldier in *Sayonara*—he has been playing quite different characters. The brute force of the man remains, the
willingness to cut through delicate problems with sledge
hammer impatience. But the controlling factor in these
characters has always been the fact that they were men in
search. All they have to go on is a dim awareness that things
should be better. In *The Wild One* no way out is offered and
the film ends in an explosion of meaningless violence. But
in *Viva Zapata* revolutionary politics offers an answer; in
Waterfront it is social consciousness; in *Sayonara* it is the
slow-coming knowledge, gained not from slogans but from

direct experience, that prejudice is a stupid limitation on man's life.

None of these answers, of course, is definitive or even earth-shakingly new. But Brando the actor gives them an importance—even, as he gropes agonizingly toward them, an excitement—which is shattering. He makes the sophisticated aware of an impolite world that sees radicalism where they have come to see only clichés. As for the younger generation, those who are Brando's age or younger, they respond to his honesty and his obvious agony.

Older generations, brought up on the notion that movie heroes should be romanticized and idealized males, remain disconcerted by the phenomenon of Brando. Perhaps they see too clearly in him the failures of the world they made. Perhaps the oft-raised cry that they do not understand him is a way of saying they understand him all too well and wish to shut out that understanding.

But this much they should admit: as a movie actor he has no peer in this generation. That he consistently underplays, yet still packs more emotion into a scene than anyone else, is a sign of a charisma that may be an act of God. But that he can grant importance to material that is frequently trivial or, at best, cheaply exciting, is a mark of the genuine actor's ability to invest bad roles with human importance. And one more thing: He does not mumble unless the role calls for it. When he does, he is good enough to communicate the emotional meaning of what he is doing, even if you can't quite hear his every word. Furthermore, the screen is the ideal medium for his style. There is no need to shout here, and no need to enunciate in the manner of a high-school forensics coach. Brando's objectives in a scene are always clear and always easy to see—if you know how to read him.

As for Brando himself, it is hard to say where he is going. He has declared that he wishes shortly to be "a has-been" as an actor so he may be free to direct. Like his screen characters, he has done much searching (his metaphor having been, chiefly, the psychoanalytic), and of late he has managed to delay unconscionably the production of two expensive films, sending them way over budget. This may be his way of getting his wish, or it may mean that he is still involved in his personal search. Whatever he finds, his efforts have struck a responsive chord in his generation. It has seen in him a child of his times, a perfect screen incarnation of its own inward gropings. So long as that is true, Brando is on safe ground when he says, "The only thing an actor owes his public is not to bore them." As things stand, he runs no such risk.

Brando, Lee J. Cobb slug it out in On the Waterfront.

With Vivian Leigh he repeats for films his great stage success in Streetcar.

Brando as directed by Brando. The star was fine, the picture (One-Eyed Jacks) not bad, but the director cost the studio more money than it felt was absolutely necessary.

Sinatra as a hired gun in Suddenly, *a cold-blooded, bravura performance.*

FROM A CAREER as a boyish, relaxed and cheerful chirper of songs for teen-agers during the war, Frank Sinatra, through sheer force of will, in 1953, converted himself, into an entirely new screen personality. His career at low ebb, both musically and on the screen, he waged a desperate war for the part of Maggio, the tragic, scrappy, funny eight-ball of *From Here to Eternity.* He played the role for an $8,000 fee, $142,000 less than his usual price. For it he won an Academy Award and a new start that has made him virtually a one-man entertainment industry.

In maturity he has become undoubtedly the finest popular singer of his time, an artist of impeccable taste. As an actor he is limited, but no less effective for his limitations. He markets a brand of bouncy toughness not unlike that of the late John Garfield, but combines it with an air of hip sophistication—he knows what the score is, he knows how to come out on top—that would have been quite beyond Garfield's tough but threatened slum kid. In this, perhaps, we see a reflection of the difference between our time and the late thirties. The economic hopelessness which formed Garfield's screen personality has disappeared. Once again, Americans are sure that anyone may rise to fame, wealth or, most important, popularity.

The fact that Sinatra's comeback was mercilessly documented in print certainly informs our vision of his screen character, as does the knowledge that in real life he is a man of mercurial moods, sudden generosity and equally sudden temper, of fierce loyalty to friends and implacable hatreds.

From Here to Eternity. *The film that turned the tide for Frank Sinatra.*

*The old Sinatra. Anchors Aweigh,
with Gene Kelly, was the best
of the many musicals Sinatra made
in the days when he played singing
sidekick to everyone on the M-G-M lot.*

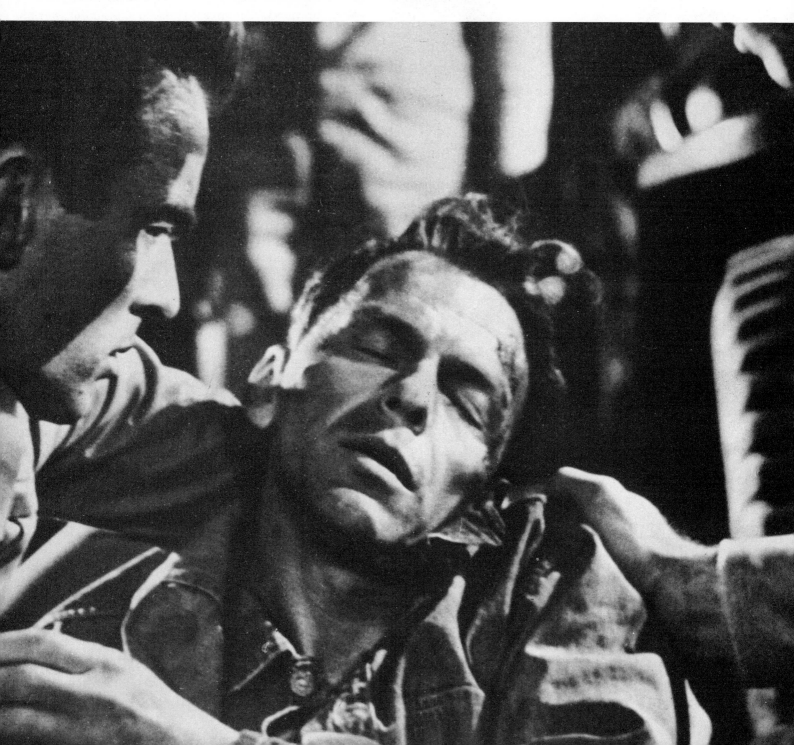

Deborah Kerr, Grace Kelly
THE NEW CLASS

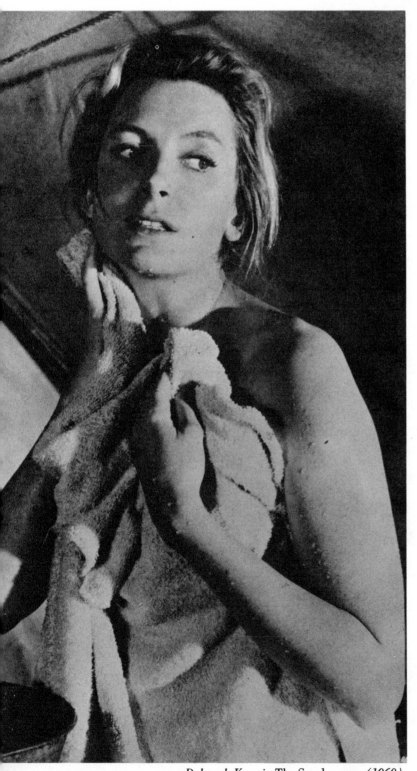

Deborah Kerr in The Sundowners *(1960)*.

FRANK SINATRA'S CAREER was not the only one revived by director Fred Zinnemann's willingness to cast against type in *From Here to Eternity*. Donna Reed, previously regarded as the perfect bourgeoise, brought this quality to the part of a whore longing for respectability and gave new depth to a standard movie role. More importantly, Miss Deborah Kerr, previously known as a glacially beautiful, terribly correct and respectable woman, suddenly manifested those qualities of fiery, desperate passion which no one before Zinnemann had the wit to tap for a screen role. The result was a triumph for Miss Kerr and yet another high point in a film which, for its perfection of tone and mood, is one of the high points of the decade's movie making, and of the new seriousness with which Hollywood was attempting to compete with television.

An English actress of classic beauty, Deborah Kerr had been playing rather frigid women since coming to Hollywood shortly after the war. Her screen character always suggested that there was more here than met the eye, that perhaps her icy manner was the result of repression rather than mere good breeding. It took the part of Karen in *Eternity* to make it clear that a real woman existed beneath that cool exterior. And, perhaps, it required new times to appreciate her womanly appeal, less blatant than that of most female stars in its blend of fire and ice.

Grace Kelly, younger, more kittenish when her defenses finally crumbled, but no less possessed of a fine beauty and a reserve that the vulgar know as "class," was the product of a wealthy and famous family, good schools, modeling and television. She made her first great impact in another Zinnemann picture, *High Noon*. In her role as an extremely ladylike Quaker, aroused finally to kill in defense of the man she loved, the public again saw the delicious combination of passion masked by coolness, reveled in the tension of waiting for the former to melt the latter. Hitchcock added the dimensions of worldliness and humor to her character in *Rear Window* and in *To Catch a Thief*.

Her career, of course, was interrupted by her royal marriage in 1956, but not before she had won an Academy Award for playing *The Country Girl*, a summation of the qualities which make up her type—reserve, morality and an underlying passion that is frequently devastating.

High Society *with John Lund.*
This remake of The Philadelphia Story *even found a*
place for Louis Armstrong.
The Swan (left), with Louis
Jourdan, was Grace Kelly's
swan song, last film before
marriage to Prince Rainier.

261

Love in the Afternoon. *Cooper was the fortunate father figure.*

As Natasha in War and Peace.

Audrey Hepburn

As Rima in Green Mansions.

"AFTER SO MANY DRIVE-IN WAITRESSES in Movies," said Billy Wilder, "here is class, somebody who went to school, can spell and possibly play the piano. . . . This girl single-handed may make bozooms a thing of the past." The director was speaking of wispy, fragile Audrey Hepburn, the little English girl who, following a New York stage debut in Colette's *Gigi*, became a full-scale movie star in *Roman Holiday* and *Sabrina*. Her kind of class was quite different from that of the Misses Kerr and Kelly. What eventually emerged from beneath their coolness was mature charm. Miss Hepburn, though fully as well bred as they were, had no coolness. Instead there is a kind of eager, coltish innocence which it is the function of her older, wiser leading men to focus and direct.

A Hepburn film begins with her scooting around in sixteen different directions, dreaming of freedom and glamour and love in the abstract. It ends with her purring contentedly in the arms of a man who has shown her that the pleasures of real love are infinitely more satisfying than those of a schoolgirl's romantic imagination. Now, other girls have played this type before, but what makes Hepburn a distinctive personality is the utter seriousness with which she seems to take herself. There is never any surface silliness in her work. Her deep, dark, ever-widening eyes seem to absorb everything which is important to the proper coming of age of Audrey Hepburn—a process so delightful that it is apparently infinitely repeatable.

Monroe and Gable in The Misfits, *Arthur Miller's hymn of love for his wife —one Marilyn Monroe.*

Bus Stop: In which the world discovered Monroe was really an actress. Arthur O'Connell co-starred.

MARILYN

THE WEEK BEFORE SHE took an overdose of sleeping pills and died, a magazine printed an interview with Marilyn Monroe in which she said: "That's the trouble, a sex symbol becomes a thing. I just hate being a thing." But because symbols are so much easier to manipulate (and to comprehend) than individuals, the world insisted that she remain one. She struggled against this fate and the record of that struggle, sometimes comic, more frequently touching, filled pages of the public prints and many moments in the conversations of ordinary people who, in more limited ways, must fight the same fight for identity. In the end, it became necessary for Marilyn Monroe to break off the unequal combat. She died the way the movie stars of fiction so frequently do, and on the morning that it happened one could find shock and sorrow but no real surprise. The symbol died with symbolic rightness. Her death had about it an air of inevitability, perhaps even of tragedy.

That tragedy was a painfully obvious one. It was, reduced to simplest terms, the story of a beautiful fantasist who suffered the construction of an ersatz personality by various experts, achieved fame as a result, and then learned that there can be no happiness when reality is flouted too long. But it is important to understand the problem in more complicated terms. She came, in time, to be her audience ("I remember when I turned to the microphone I looked all the way up and back and I thought, 'That's where I'd be—way up there under the rafters, close to the ceiling, after I'd paid my $2 to come into the place.' "). It takes a stronger mind than she possessed to be an image, an observer of the image, and a person in her own right. A few stars have been the successful executive presiding over an alienated self which is but a product. She was not one of them.

But she did not do badly. She learned that "sexuality is only attractive when it's natural and spontaneous" and somehow she was able to give us a vision of sex and pleasure that was direct, honest, funny but unsniggering. In the end she and her admirers and advisors sought to wrap the respectable cloak of art about her presence. In the context of her times, this may have seemed necessary, but it should be firmly noted that her natural presence was its own reward, her ability to project it freely something beyond mere artifice and quite aside from art. Perhaps her best epitaph is a line from Auden's memorial poem to Yeats: "You were silly like us; your gift survived it all."

The quintessential Marilyn as photographed by Richard Avedon.

Two aspects of Moses as conceived by Heston and director Cecil B. DeMille.

CHARLTON HESTON

Trusty, brave, clean and <u>reverent</u>

AT FIRST, EVERYONE THOUGHT Charlton Heston was under-acting. Reviewing his first film, Bosley Crowther of the New York *Times* found in him "a quiet but assertive magnetism, a youthful dignity." Three years later, *Variety* was noting that one of his performances was "forthright, steely-eyed" and that "he has a superb manner of underplaying through voice and a minimum of gestures."

Then came the string of spectacles in super-duper scope, *The Greatest Show on Earth, The Ten Commandments, The Big Country, Ben-Hur, El Cid,* and all of a sudden it began occurring to people that Heston was acting with all the passion at his command, that the curiously lifeless gestures and the general stiffness of his demeanor were about all he could manage and that, oddly, they were priceless commodities. He in no way interfered with the expensive scenery, the mobs of people, the general air of expensive expansiveness that are the real stars of a movie spectacle. In addition, he has the physical stature and presence not to be overwhelmed by a film of huge scope. He is, as someone suggested, the Francis X. Bushman of his time.

Which is not quite fair to Heston. For he is a serious, sincere and intelligent individual who has repeatedly made financial sacrifices in order to broaden his acting range. He accepted considerably less than his usual fee in order to work under Orson Welles' direction in *Touch of Evil,* a small, gamey, superbly sadistic murder melodrama; he attempted a dreadful Broadway play, *The Juggler,* in order to work under Laurence Olivier's direction. "I don't want to get stuck doing one thing," he has said. "Once the public gets you pegged you can't escape."

Heston claims he has wanted to act since he was five years old and played Santa Claus in a school production. He studied theater at Northwestern University and, while there, appeared in a remarkable 16-mm. film of *Julius Caesar* which he and his fellow students shot in and around Chicago—of all places. A few parts on Broadway in the late forties led directly to Hollywood and film stardom.

It may be that he is too intelligent to do the kind of subtle, emotional acting that is the essence of good screen work. In any event, it is his misfortune to be rather noble in appearance and, hence, to be a natural choice for roles requiring an aristocratic bearing. He himself has said that some actors seem to have faces that belong to certain historical eras. William Holden, he says, is the perfect modern American, Henry Fonda the perfect antebellum American, Bogart the urban American. And what is Heston's historical era? "Apparently somewhere before Christ," he says a little sadly.

ROCK HUDSON *The constructed hero*

Hudson in hot pursuit of Lollobrigida in Come September.

"I THINK," ROCK HUDSON has been heard to say, "that I'm rather average." In terms of talent, the statement is certainly true enough. Despite a recently discovered—and quite modest—ability to play light comedy, it has to be said that his chief attribute seems to be a rather dogged determination to do the right thing. By dint of constant effort, which makes one uncomfortable, the way unnatural things do, he gets through his parts. In comedies like *Pillow Talk* and *Lover Come Back*, shrewd directors have made his unease a comic virtue, and his good-natured goofiness, while hardly a challenge to Cary Grant, is quite amusing. But in serious roles, Hudson communicates nothing so much as strain. Since he is really too pretty to be believed as a Western hero, that traditional refuge of the non-actor is denied him.

Still, average though his talent may be, Hudson's road to stardom was exceptional. A truck driver, he habitually parked near studio gates, arranged himself against a fender and awaited discovery. It was agent Henry Willson, a specialist in oddly named leading men for the teen-age market,

who guided him upward. Observing Roy Fitzgerald's massive proportions and rather slow ways of speech and movement, this unacclaimed genius found his thoughts turning to things as steadfast as the Rock of Gibraltar, as majestic as the Hudson River. Thus did Willson achieve his greatest triumph of nomenclature.

Hudson came to greatness—if that is the word for it—in the faceless fifties, when the demand for oddly angled personalities, particularly among the teen-agers (increasingly the majority of moviegoers), reached its lowest point. Hudson's screen personality, rubbed down by a hundred eager craftsmen, was polished as smooth as a piece of sandstone worn by the river whose name he bore. In a way, he was dehumanized. He became an everyman who was also a nobody—a kind of generalized dream American. In a way it is too bad; there has to be something interesting about a fellow who attempts to get discovered the way Hudson did. One would have liked to know the young man leaning against that truck.

268

The Number One box-office attraction (male) gives the screen's Number One box-office attraction (female) a lift. The film is Pillow Talk.

Shirley MacLaine's first movie, the charming The Trouble with Harry.

The new breed SHIRLEY MACLAINE

ONE MAGAZINE CALLED ROCK HUDSON a "stolid gold invest-ment," and as a kind of least-common-denominator hero he achieved, late in the decade, a steady place as the films' top box-office attraction. But the decade produced more in-teresting phenomena than Hudson and his ilk. There was, for instance, a marvelously kookie girl named Shirley MacLaine, a sometime chorine and understudy in Broadway musicals. Replacing an ailing star, she was spotted by Alfred Hitchcock, who cast her in a hilarious shaggy-dog story called *The Trouble with Harry* (1954), very likely the best film Hitchcock did during the decade. It was, to put it mild-ly, a picture for people of special tastes, but Miss MacLaine's totally distracted, deadpan performance was a wonder. In-side of five years, her salary went from $6,000 to $250,000 per picture.

Possessed of a beautifully leggy form and a childlike, re-markably expressive face, she is a direct, spontaneous and completely natural actress. "In front of the cameras I have to be careful what I think," she has said, "because it all shows." In a button-down age, she is completely—though not insistently—uninhibited, and it may be a measure of the time's repressiveness that a woman who is simply her-self should come to seem something of an eccentric. Miss MacLaine's appeal was best summed up by a producer who said, "Everything she does is real, the way she picks up a pen or a cup of coffee, the way she eats a sandwich." "She has," adds a director, "the honesty of a person living each moment as it happens."

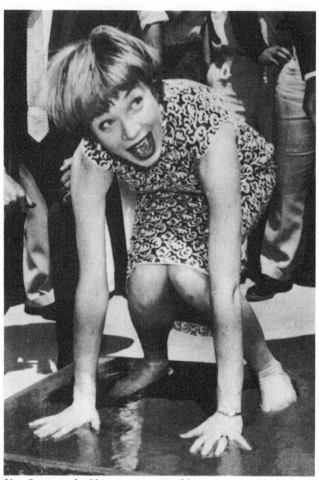

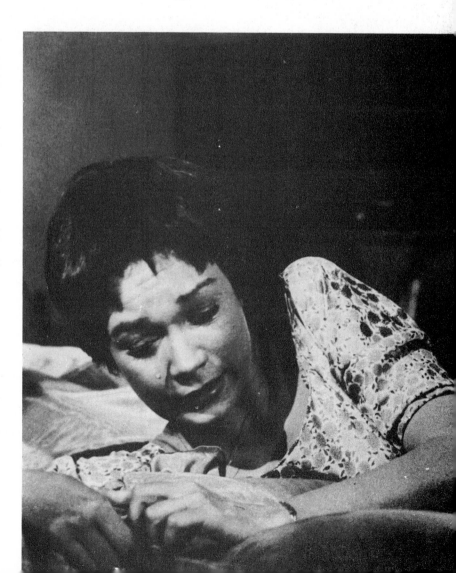

Not Grauman's Chinese, just a publicity stunt for the Indianapolis Speedway. Right, as she appeared in Hot Spell.

The new breed JACK LEMMON

The Bright Young Man on the rise, thanks to The Apartment.

JACK LEMMON'S COMEDY is that of quiet desperation, and it is possible that his screen personality will someday seem to be the comic quintessence of his age. For he is superbly, supremely the new American, college educated, an organization man, trying gamely to retain the old American values, yet still striving for a secure place within the oversystematized system.

The essence of Lemmon's screen presence was demonstrated in a scene in *The Apartment*. He is at his anonymous junior-executive desk, one of hundreds in a huge, factorylike room. He has a terrible cold which he is fighting with Kleenex, pills, a nasal inhaler. But it is necessary, without calling attention to himself and without seeming anxious or angry, to rearrange the schedule of executives who have taken to using his apartment for illicit romantic rendezvous. Armed with an appointment pad, a Rolodex, a telephone and all the clichés of polite business usage, he begins to elicit their cooperation in his changed plans. The scene is a vicious parody of the manners and

morals of the business community by a man who loathes its ways yet must live with them. His cruel dilemma is explored and exploited in a piece of acting that is one of the small gems of recent years.

Lemmon is, in background, very like the Bright Young Men he plays so well. He was educated in prep schools and at Harvard, and he was a junior officer in the Navy. Thereafter, he turned to acting and scored his first successes in television. His first movie role as a characteristically eager and sincere young man, was *It Should Happen to You* (1954). As a serious actor he is caught in a dilemma very like that which might plague one of his characters. He told an interviewer about the perils of success: "Suddenly you find that you're only giving two performances a year. You're a success as an actor, but vast limitations have been placed in your work. If you defy the system—take a character role, as many fine actors in England do—then you're not a star any more, and the best pictures won't be offered to you."

The Bright Young Man at play, or at least trying hard.

The old magic SOPHIA LOREN

"IN SPITE OF HAVING THE USUAL womanly defects," says Vittorio De Sica, "she is the only really spiritually honest woman I have ever known." Thus, Sophia Loren, a woman whose beauty is triumphantly greater than the sum of its parts, a poor Italian child who in the space of a few years has become not merely a world-wide object of desire but an actress of considerable depth. If our taste in love goddesses is shifting away from glamorous emptiness, then Sophia Loren is both product and instigator of that shift.

In effect, she is a Hollywood star, since nearly all of her films are financed by the American industry, but her best work has been done in the movies which the industry has filmed elsewhere. Run-away production threatens the existence of Hollywood as a film capital, but it may be the salvation of its vitality as a creative force. The films Sophia Loren made there are uniformly strained, cliché-ridden, and artificial. The pictures she has made elsewhere have, for the most part, allowed her to be her fiery, humorous, deeply sensual self.

She is seen best in a natural light. A natural wonder, after all, needs no re-enforcement by an architect. Says De Sica: "Sophia is a typical result of today's Italian cinema. She represents the artistic expression we look for, the lack of speculation based on effects. The American cinema, with all its mechanism, is no more than an industry. Art doesn't enter into it. Our cinema is more precarious, but our people have individualism."

It is a fact that Miss Loren retains her individuality yet manages to be a universal symbol of the desirability of the unaffected, completely natural woman. That is the key to her sudden emergence as the foremost leading lady of our time. She is the very opposite of what the European woman used to represent in the movies. There is nothing vampish about her, and parenthetically we may note that the European woman has, since the war, come to represent a new sexual ideal—unteasing directness. Miss Loren does not tease. One knows that she will keep her promise of delight.

The Fabulous Feline in a playful humor.

Loren as she appeared in It Happened in Naples, *a fairy tale about an alley cat who dared look at The King—Clark Gable.*

The old magic TONY CURTIS

"Match me, Sidney." Sweet Smell of Success *was one of Curtis' best.*

The bad old days—The Black Shield of Falworth.

THERE IS A STORY, possibly apocryphal, of a young man named Bernie Schwartz, who most desperately wanted to be an actor. As a child in the Bronx, he had been permanently but charmingly seduced by incessant attendance at the neighborhood movie house. As a sailor during World War II, he had nurtured his dream of being a dashing star through the long, dull watches of submarine duty. Mustered out, he became a hanger-on with a young comedian then working with Perry Como. Emerging one night from a theater, Como was surrounded by a mob of squealing fans who, in their eagerness, even thrust their autograph books at Schwartz, who began delightedly to scribble away. "Hey, kid, what are you doing? You're not even in show business," cried the bemused Como. "I'm trying, I'm trying," shouted Schwartz.

Not long afterward he found himself under contract to Universal-International pictures, and the transformation of Bernie Schwartz to Tony Curtis began at the last studio to retain a genuine program for the training of young talent. "I was a million-to-one shot," Curtis now says, "the least likely to succeed. I wasn't low man on the totem pole, I was

under the totem pole, in a sewer, tied in the sack." But that tough, cheerful eagerness that has became his screen essence endeared him to many on the lot—among them the publicity man. Curtis found himself in parts consisting of no more than saying "Woo-woo" but, thanks to the P.R. men, a star as far as the youthful readers of the fan magazines were concerned. They built up tremendous pressure for him, capped by a mob scene at a San Francisco theater where he was making a personal appearance. This led him into a string of program pictures which no one but the kids took seriously. He played cowboys and caliphs with his Bronx accent, then went into a series of films with distinguished stars.

"I educated my fans," he says. "They began to say to themselves, 'Well, Burt Lancaster don't play scenes with bums.' " He also educated the highbrows. In pictures like *Sweet Smell of Success* he projected a tough, nervously energetic quality that separated him from his more placid contemporaries and suddenly caused the critics to notice him. Now, more than able to carry a film by himself, he is a strangely appealing, old fashioned star.

Tony Curtis and Sidney Poitier in The Defiant Ones.

ELIZABETH TAYLOR *The last star*

The beginnings of stardom. Little Liz in National Velvet.

ELIZABETH TAYLOR RECEIVES the highest salary any actor has ever attained. It is fitting, for since the age of eight Miss Taylor has had no identity but as an actress or, more accurately, as a public personality. For good or ill, her entire life has been devoted to living a dream peculiar to her time and place. She was even so unlucky as to have no adolescent awkward age which would have given her respite, however temporary, from life in public. In short, she was, is and will forever be a movie star. There is no other significant fact to record about her life—for that fact has informed nearly every waking moment of her every day.

George Stevens, the director for whom she gave two of her best performances (in *A Place in the Sun* and in *Giant*), has said that "She was kept in a cocoon by her mother, by her studio, by the fact that she was the adored child who had had everything she wanted since she was eight years old. What most people don't know is that there has been a smoldering spirit of revolt in Elizabeth for a long time."

Her mother had once had a modest acting career herself, but it had been cut short by her marriage to Francis Taylor, an art dealer. Eventually they settled in Los Angeles. "It was almost impossible to believe—finding myself in the film capital with my children," said Mrs. Taylor. She determinedly set about making them into stars. Elizabeth's brother, Howard, would have none of it. He went so far as to shave his head on the eve of one screen test.

Elizabeth, however, was not so strong—though she has frequently placed on public record her admiration for her brother's independence. She had one small part at Universal before her option was dropped. Then, in 1942, during a blackout, her air raid warden father fell into conversation with a fellow warden, producer Sam Marx, who was looking for a child to appear opposite Roddy MacDowell in *Lassie Come Home*. Elizabeth read for the part and got it. Two years later, at age twelve, she had the lead in the memorable *National Velvet*.

Two years after that she could have played a mature woman. Even as a child star she had a fascinating air of

The princess awakens. Montgomery Clift, Elizabeth Taylor, A Place in the Sun.

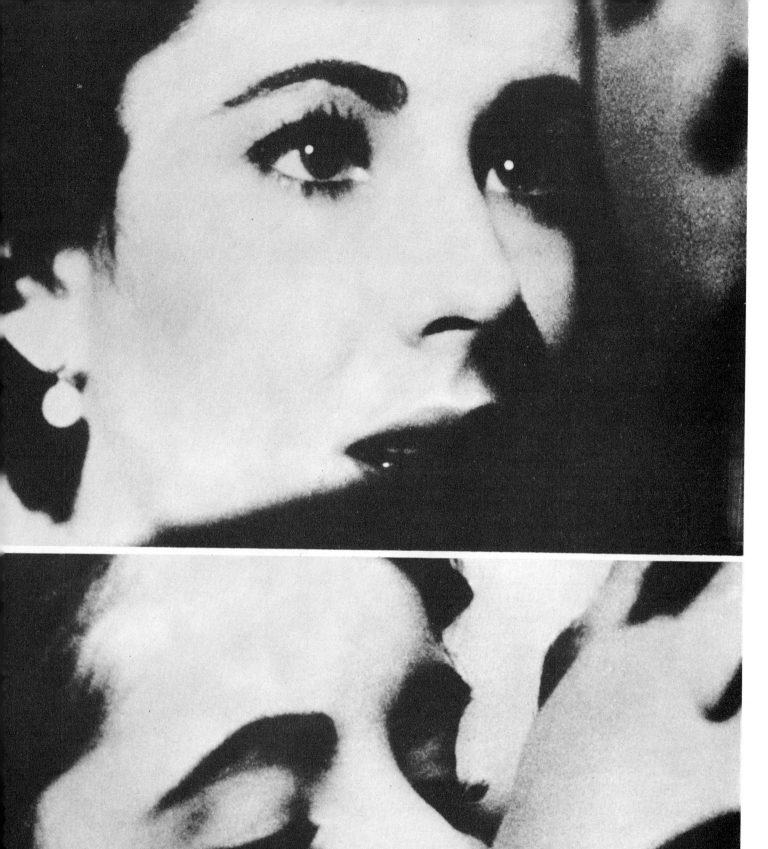

experience about her. The casting director who had dropped her said, "Her eyes are too old. She doesn't have the face of a kid." It is a quality which has persisted, a major part of the excitement she creates, though now the eyes give the illusion not of age but of ageless womanly wisdom.

In the forties and fifties Elizabeth Taylor endured, though it could not be said that she prevailed. She began to hate the Hollywood that had robbed her of her childhood, sullenly played her parts with no more than rudimentary grace. She could not act, she could only give the illusion of existence. Cast as a willful child-woman, the natural development of the womanly child she had been, she was adequate, but it was her perfect beauty that kept her steadily, uninterestingly, before the cameras.

Then came her marriage to Mike Todd. "More than anyone realizes, Mike was responsible for the intellectual and emotional awakening of this girl," director Joseph Mankiewicz said. "For all his flamboyance, he was a man of an infinite variety of interests . . . she had been a sort of Sleeping Beauty in an isolated castle. Mike took her through the cobweb to the other world. . . ."

In touch with reality of a sort, Elizabeth Taylor began to add new dimensions to her screen presence. Her roles were very much in the mode that had become customary for her, but now they were touched by life—especially after the deeply felt tragedy of Todd's death in a plane crash. The rest is current history—the loss of public affection when she broke up the Eddie Fisher–Debbie Reynolds marriage, the regaining of that affection (and an Academy Award) in the sentimental orgy surrounding her near death in London, the epochal off-screen romance during the making of *Cleopatra* and the ending of her marriage to Fisher. In her work she may now be able to touch reality as never before. But her life itself, that curious compound of legend and unreality, will never seem anything but a fantasy, an inextricable tangle of the real and the unreal which she, least of all, seems capable of sorting out.

In a sense, Elizabeth Taylor is a reversion to the superromantic stars of the silent screen, deliberately out of touch with common mortality. If that is true, then there will never be another movie star like her, for the system that produced them and, in its dying hours, produced Elizabeth Taylor, is now gone forever.

The actress awakens. Elizabeth Taylor, Paul Newman, Cat on a Hot Tin Roof.

PERHAPS THE SYMBOLS ARE TOO OBVIOUS: Chaplin at the beginning of his career, tremulously eager, awaiting a gift from the sea; James Mason in the 1954 remake of *A Star is Born* wading into the same sea to commit suicide. Playing a fading star in a fading industry, Mason, in this scene from a romantic and sentimental film—pure Hollywood—provides the coda to our study of that most peculiar of democratic social institutions, the movie star. As institutions go, it has had a short life.

There will be, doom-sayers to the contrary, at least another fifty years of stars. Individuals will dominate the screen as dictatorially as any in the past. They will attain those heights of celebrity which, in our democratic fashion, we so mightily deprecate and envy. But these stars will not be stars of the movies alone. They will exercise their talents (or, if they have none, their primal appeals) in a wide variety of media. They will, as never before, be the masters of their own fate and, with studio system virtually destroyed, it will be less possible to fabricate a personality for a beautiful dope. Tastes being what they are these days, stars may even have to do more acting, in the conventional meaning of the term, than they ever did.

The late Buddy Adler saw doom in the naturalism which has been creeping across Hollywood in the last fifteen years. "We're dealing in illusion," he said, "and when the Elizabeth Taylors and Marilyn Monroes start to think and want to live normal lives like everyone else, soon we won't have any illusions left to sell." But Adler reckoned without democracy, especially as we have known it since 1932. Your true democrat is more interested in processes than in product, enjoys being privy to illusions. Somehow, the knowledge that it is all done with mirrors makes him even more eager to surrender his disbelief at the box office. The democratization of movie stardom is a long-term trend, and it will continue. There will, in future, be fewer of them, but they will continue to exist. We need them. THE END

282

INDEX

286